AT THE FIRESIDE
～ VOL. 3 ～

DEBBY
MY *CARIAD*

WHEN YOUR SUN
ROSE UPON MY PERSON'AL HORIZON
I COULD ONLY BASK IN ITS GLORY.

IT SHARPENED MY ABILITY TO SEE
IT WARMED THE VERY DEPTH OF MY SOUL.

SPIRITS LIKE YOU
SHOULD BE CLONED

AND SCATTERED
THROUGHOUT OUR UNIVERSE.

AT THE FIRESIDE
~ VOL. 3 ~
TRUE SOUTHERN AFRICAN STORIES

Roger Webster
Foreword by Max du Preez

Published by Spearhead
An imprint of New Africa Books (Pty) Ltd.
99 Garfield Road
Claremont 7700
South Africa

(021) 674 4136
info@newafricabooks.co.za

Copyright in text © Roger Webster 2005
Copyright in published edition © Spearhead 2005

All rights reserved. No part of this publication may be reproduced or transmitted in any form or by any means without prior written permission from the publisher.

First edition, first impression 2005

ISBN: 0-86486-582-1

Edited by Mark McClellan
Project management by Cherie Wright
Proofreading by Patricia Myers Smith
Design by Peter Stuckey
Typesetting by Mckore Graphics
Cover design by Toby Newsome
Printing and binding by Shumani Printers

Contents

Foreword vii
Death of the Zulu 1
African cosmology 5
The myth makers 8
Coenraad de Buys – the early years 11
The Battle of Boomplaats 16
The Battle of Khunwana 19
Penduka safaris 21
The Elephant House 24
Forgotten tribes of the Gatsrand 26
The baboon of Uitenhage 29
Sir Harry Smith 31
The *Alabama* 39
Changes leading to chaos and conflict 42
The Limpopo Province 44
Nomansland 46
An ancient South African battle 49
Lüderitzbucht 52
Old timers 55
Casualties of war 58
How the Milky Way was formed 60
Modern-day Botswana 63
David Livingstone 66
Death of a chief 78
Big-hearted men and little boats 81

Birth of a mining town 84
Siener van Rensburg 87
Potter's Hill 90
The *Grosvenor* and her castaways 93
The Magabeng – Part 1 102
The Magabeng – Part 2 105
Constance Vivian 108
The missionary station of Genadendal 121
Murder most foul 123
The Eastern Cape 126
The oaks of the fair Cape 129
The saddle 132
The true settlers 136
Thirst for the past 139
A historical swindle 142
God's finger 145
'She who walks by moonlight' 149
Bibliography 155

Foreword

Of course we need historians of the academic variety. Someone needs to search for and analyse dusty old documents and teach these skills to university students. But history can't just be an academic pursuit. We need storytellers to make history come alive, to bring history to the citizens. Storytellers like Roger Webster.

More than a decade after the advent of democracy, South Africans still struggle to understand each other. They attack and defend from racial, ethnic, group or regional enclosures. They find it hard to understand why others behave in the way they do. They still wrestle with identity. These things happen because most South Africans still have a very poor understanding of their past.

Part of the reason for this is the way we have been taught history at school. It mostly consisted of an endless array of grey men, wars and conquests in far-off lands, and a lot of dates. History became like soggy, over-cooked cabbage – boring and bland – but teachers insisted it was good for you.

Roger Webster has done more than most in South Africa to serve up history as a tantalising dish: oxtail and mieliepap, bobotie and yellow rice, prawn curry and green salad, served with a good red wine and often with a shot of mampoer to finish it off.

Roger's history is not populated by ideologies, presidents and prime ministers, conquering armies and sets of legislation. It is populated by human beings, warm-blooded people with personalities and emotions. They love and they hate, they're scared and they're brave, they're jealous and proud. They're heroes and villains and scoundrels and everything in-between. They're real. They're just like us. And that's why we can relate to them and understand what they did and how that affects us now. They're individuals before they are members of racial or ethnic or class groups.

Roger is not only a good storyteller; he is passionate about it. His passion and love for stories from our past have touched tens of thousands of people through his books, his radio talks, his conversations with groups and individuals. In the good old African tradition of storytelling, Roger has an eye for the unexpected angle, a nose for the story behind the story.

Make no mistake: Roger is not a history professor, but few professional historians have his wide-ranging knowledge and broad understanding of history. I still have to meet one with Roger's sense of adventure to dig up more stories and insights.

May there be many Roger Webster books after this one.

Max du Preez
Author: *Of Warriors, Lovers and Prophets*

Death of the Zulu

I was standing in a mega-supermarket the other day, watching the hundreds of items beep through the tills, when I realised that we have been robbed of time. I remember a time when the checkout clerk had to first look at the price, then manually punch it in, then place the item down and pick up the next one. The same era in which, when you went to the grocer or the butcher, he used to write all the prices on the sheet of brown paper to add up your bill. Maybe it was an era when we had more time – when we didn't scream around in our motorcars and suffer from road rage – because we gave time to one another and didn't snatch it for ourselves.

In our no-time era I think we have lost the ability to pause and understand each other as human beings. Our very own Uys Krige, captured by the Germans during the Second World War, wrote a story that beautifully illustrates this point and it concerns the death of a Zulu:

'It was about two hours after our capture that we were marching from Fig Tree to Tobruk. It was mid-summer and the sun was up, and we were trudging along that bone-dry earth. We weren't doing anything, not even thinking, simply trudging and dragging our heavy feet through the sand. I appeared to have two minds, the one stunned and without feeling, the other perfectly conscious. To survive the vacuum of battle, you have to live in the now. You have no past, which reminds you of your wife and of your children, and you cannot have a future. So you are trapped in the now.

'There were dead bodies lying beside the road, some singly and some in batches. I didn't look. I wasn't interested. As we rounded a curve, I heard a shout. I looked up and there, 50 yds away, stood a German officer standing over somebody stretched out on the ground. He shouted again and beckoned with his arms. He wants me – I thought. He is looking straight at me. I went across. The next minute I was standing beside the man lying on the ground. It was one of our South African native soldiers, and I could see by his build that he was a Zulu. I knew the language from working in Natal for a long time. Then I saw his eyes. Luminous, jet black and stricken with pain. He was looking straight at me, yet he appeared unaware of my presence.

'"*Yini mfana* – What is it young Zulu?" I asked and, bending over him, I really didn't want to be there. My present mind was saying, "Leave me alone." When he heard his own language, he came back.

'"*Hawu! ... Mlungu kubi*," he groaned "*ngishaywe yinsimbi*." – "White man, the iron has hit me."

'"How do you feel *mfana*?"

'A hard glitter came into his eyes.

'"*Mlungu, ngidubule!*" – "White man, shoot me!"

'"Don't talk like that *mfana*. You have only lost an arm, many men have lost arms, you will walk again in the sun."

'"*Cha ... Cha*," – "No, No," he muttered, almost angrily.

'I looked down at the blood-clotted stump which used to be his right forearm, and I could see the cut marks across the right side of his khaki shirt that had been ripped by the tiny bits of shrapnel.

'"I'll get you a doctor and you will be healthy and strong again, and you will be back amongst your people in Zululand and you will be doing all the things that you used to do. You will sow again and you will make beer," I told him.

'"*Cha mlungu ngidubule*," he replied."

'He looked at me with his steely eyes that I had seen so many times amongst the old Zulu Ndunas, with the depth of knowledge that came from ancient African wisdom "*Kuphelile okwami*" ... "I am finished."

'A desert car drove up 20 yds away and a tall, thin German officer with sharp features came across and he bent over the native, feeling his chest beneath the blood-stiffened shirt. I noticed the stars and the two entwined snakes of Aesculapius on his badge and I was greatly relieved.

'"*Ngidubule*," he said again.

'"You speak foolish things," I said to him.

'When I looked at his body, I remembered that the Zulu men are some of the most physically beautiful people in the world and they have such extraordinary pride in their physique that they consider any deformity of the body – and particularly disfigurement – as something unnatural – even monstrous. Formerly, they killed all children unfortunate enough to be born as cripples.

'"*Ngidubule mlungu*" – it was almost a command now.

'"What does he say?" asked the German.

'"It is his request that we shoot him."

'He was leaning up against me now – his whole left arm supporting his body. He turned to the German – "*Wena ngidubule*."

'"He wants you to shoot him, because I can't," I said.

'The doctor touched my arm – "Perhaps it is the simplest way out. God only knows how he survived with that loss of blood and, if we move him, he will die."

'And the German doctor handed me his Luger. "My business is to preserve life," he said, "not to destroy it."

'"*Ngidubule*" … the voice rang in my ears.

'"No," I said, handing it back to him, "I cannot shoot my friends."

'The next moment the Captain handed the pistol back to the owner.

'"Herr Oberleutnant Müller," he rapped out in military tone, "Shoot this man."

'I looked at the Zulu, and a smile came across his face. He didn't understand the German command, but he knew exactly what it meant. He somehow managed to lift his arm and rip open his torn khaki shirt, revealing his chest, and on the right hand side was just a mass of torn flesh. I felt a hand clutch my shoulder. It was the Lieutenant, and it was a long way away, in my head, that I heard the single crack of that Luger. I sat there on the side of the road, and many, many legs passed me by; slipping in and out of my vision. I just sat there staring at my boots. Eventually, someone shouted in Afrikaans – "Come along Du Toit, come along" – and when I found myself again, I was once more amongst that crowd, tramping slowly and wearily as prisoners do, towards Tobruk. Back in the now. But somehow I had a deeper understanding of the immense pride of my people in Zululand.'

African cosmology

As we progress into the new South Africa, many parts of our history that were buried or conveniently forgotten are starting to emerge. One part that I particularly like is the references to the use of the stars in ancient times.

It is starting to be known that the old people of this ancient land had quite a thorough knowledge of the southern night skies, and the influences that the various planets had upon the climate of the country. For instance, when Pleiades, or the constellation of the Seven Sisters, was in a certain position, it would be the time for harvesting, and when Orion was ascendant it would be time for the summer rains.

Richard Wade, a friend of mine, has undertaken a great deal of research in this field and his findings are quite remarkable. As an example, he relates the night skies and the major planets of our solar system to the alignment of the Great Zimbabwe Ruins. When Richard superimposed the sky-watch programme of the southern hemisphere onto the ruins of Zimbabwe on the night of the mid-year solstice – 22 June – he was not too surprised to find that the plinths on the north-facing wall of the ruins aligned perfectly with five of our solar system's planets. The possibility of this being coincidental is mathematically negligible. This means that someone with a knowledge of the solar system had placed them there deliberately. Who? We don't know. But I think that the why is slowly becoming obvious, for the changing of the seasons affected everybody's lives and it was of great importance to know when to plant, when to reap, when to be joyous and when to weep.

Let's consider the time to be joyous. The young women, particularly of the BaVenda, will gather together with the tribe and celebrate the now famous Domba: the Dance of the Python. With the drums beating and the older women singing, these young maidens link up their elbows one behind the other and, in an hypnotic motion of two steps forward to the left and two steps forward to the right, snake their way through this magnificent ritual. It is a rite marking the end of pubescence and the beginning of fertile life for these emerging women. The dance is dedicated to Naledi, or Venus, the Goddess of Fertility. I don't think it could be a coincidence that the African Goddess of Fertility happens to be Venus, her Roman equivalent. The coincidence is too great. For, you see, the orbital time of Venus in its path around the Sun is exactly the same number of days as the gestation or pregnancy period of the human female. Coincidence? I don't think so.

So when the world stopped to look at the Goddess of Fertility slowly going across the face of the Sun [8 June 2004], an old bushman poem came to mind:

Venus and the Sun
or
Naledi and the Universal God of the Sky

And, as we stood there, quietly watching,
Our eyes were dimmed with reverence for the ritual.
I saw the Goddess of Fertility get up
And start to walk across the face of the God of the Universe.
She slowly walked across his face,
Absorbing his life-giving light
And showing all that watched
That the sacred union between the two was still there
And that the Life Forces, where we are,
Would continue.
She walked off his face
And the Life Force did continue
Just a little better than before.

I, for one, particularly wonder, as we start unravelling this beautiful history of what the old people called the 'dark continent', just how much more we are going to discover and re-discover of that ancient knowledge.

The myth makers

Western culture is steeped in *logos* – rational thought processes. More ancient cultures and belief systems, including those of the indigenous tribes of Africa, are instead immersed in the notion of *mythos* – an internal, subconscious reality that transcends the confines of empirical rationalism.

This myth-based reality meant, for example, the ancients believed (just like the European pagans of old) that the Earth was a female, hence the expression 'Mother Earth'. They also believed that it was not dissimilar to the female ovum, and so, when it rained they likened the millions of droplets that were falling from the (male) sky to the sperm of the male. And as this male rain fell upon the female ovum so the earth would become fertilized and grow an abundance of various things. (This so-called 'heathen thinking' occurred in a people who had never even heard of the terms 'education' or 'schooling'. Nevertheless, it represents a point of view which modern science is now beginning to concede may be justifiable after all.)

These ingrained beliefs meant that everything who was linked to the fertility and reproduction of the Earth-Mother was regarded as 'female business' and could not be tampered with in any way, shape or form by the male. Interference would result in horrifying punishments, including the destruction of yourself and your entire family. So men left Mother Earth well alone.

Now comes the white man, into a world that is being driven more and more by *logos* – the logical – and the old mythological ways and beliefs are being pushed further and further into the past. We have invented the wheel, our ships float on the oceans and we are 'discovering' the world.

We have ploughs and have harnessed and tamed the horse and ox; we have enslaved the aboriginal tribes with gunpowder, rifle, cannon and cheap liquor, so now they must till the soil to bring forth the grain.

When it was politely explained to the missionaries and settlers that it was not the place of the male to interfere with the doings of the Earth-Mother, and that those were things pertaining to women only, they scoffed. The people doing the explaining were told that their belief structure was rubbish, then beaten into submission until they were forced to work the land, knowing full well that they were condemning their families forever. This is exactly where the belief in black men being 'lazy' originated. The black m[...]

[newspaper clipping obscures text:
kcrow@plaind.com, 216-999-4046
Previous columns online:
cleveland.com/crow.
Hear Crow at 8:20 a.m. every Wednesday on WDOK FM/102.1. And if you're not sick of her yet, check out her blog at www.blog.cleveland.com/style.]

In [...] 1900s, Dorethea van Bleek, along with her doctor father, learnt the language of the Bushmen who were enslaved and used to build the breakwater for the Cape Town harbour. These Bushmen, mainly from the Kenhardt district of the Northern Cape, related their beliefs and mythology to the doctor and his daughter, who faithfully recorded them for posterity. They are considered to be the most definitive records of these people.

One of the Bushmen's stories, which absolutely fascinates me, is the one they called 'The Jewel of the Night'. They said that he rose in the morning and that he loved the Earth-Mother so much that he would look at her face six times, while she showed him her face but once. He would always be in the company of only one child, and this is the way it would always be.

Some decades before 1930 mathematicians had calculated that there were two planets in our solar system in addition to the seven already known to exist. They were not visible from Earth with the naked eye, and the scholars pinpointed them by the effect that they had on the orbits of the other planets. In 1846, T G Galle, working at the Berlin Observatory, confirmed the existence of an eighth planet, which was named Neptune. In 1930, the first photograph of this planet were taken and another plant, named Pluto, was also discovered and photographed. Pluto rotates on its axis six times faster than Earth – thereby showing its face six times to the Earth's once, just as the Bushman myth described it!

In 1978, it was discovered that Pluto had a single satellite orbiting it; they named this 'Charon' – what the Bushmen called the planet's 'one child'.

These plants were invisible to the naked eye. How come the Bushmen spoke of them in their mythology? Was information that we have only recently been privy to handed down from generation to generation, in a time when a lot more was known than we have knowledge of? Is this a case of *logos* slowly catching up with *mythos*? I don't have the answers, but I do know one thing: the more I look into things of this nature, the more I begin to wonder.

Coenraad de Buys – the early years

Coenraad de Buys was born in 1761. His mother, Christina, named him after his grandfather, Coenraad Scheepers. Christina had three husbands in her lifetime. The second was Jean du Buis the Third, the son of Jean du Buis the Second who was quite a wealthy man and possessed a total of nine slaves. The Du Buis family did not approve of his marriage to Christina. As a consequence, all the couple received upon their betrothal was a wagon and a span of oxen.

Christina and Du Buis lived some 250 km east of Cape Town on a river the Bushmen called the Gouritz. The Boers at that time kept moving further and further eastwards, because, for 24 rix dollars, one could rent 6 000 acres of land from the government. What could be a simpler way of feeding cattle or sheep than simply moving to new, cheap pasture whenever the need arose? When the Boers encountered resilient Bushmen or Hottentots, they would exterminate the menfolk and incorporate the women for breeding and the children for labour. And, of course, the further away from Cape Town one moved, the further away from the taxes and controls of the Dutch East India Company one was (though the company did move eastwards in an attempt to reassert its influence).

When the Dutch government of the Cape decreed, a hundred years earlier, that slaves could be imported from west and east Africa, India, Java, Madagascar, Macassar and Malacca, two significant changes occurred in the country. Firstly, it became shameful for a white man to use his hands in physical toil; this was the work of the slaves – the Hottentots and Bushmen. The slaves and servants ploughed and harvested, tended livestock and generally undertook all the arduous tasks that their white masters demanded of them.

For the Bushmen, an ancient race who had roamed the lands originally, this change brought about their eventual destruction. These gentle, talented people – renowned for their astonishing rock painting – were incorporated into other tribes, and their blood lived on only in the bodies of others. Even more tragically they were often shot on sight, regarded by both whites and blacks as vermin to be exterminated.

Gradually, both the Bushmen and the Hottentots started losing their land to the whites, by barter or by bullet, and became, in effect, 'owned' by the new occupiers.

The second profound change that the slave economy brought about was the mixing of tribes and races. White blood first mixed with slave blood when transient soldiers and sailors took women from the government's slave houses for their sexual pleasure and satisfaction. Furthermore, white farmers often took slave women in order to breed a new supply of labourers. The law stated that slave children were the property of the slave owner and so, from the age of seven, these children would begin to perform menial tasks in and around the farm. Modern historical accounts also fail to acknowledge the fact that white men, desiring homes but without the means to marry white women, took solace in the less demanding, and therefore 'available', Cape girls.

Two distinct types of people developed. One – a mixture of Hottentot, White, African and Malay – was a yellow, full-eyed, prominent featured, straight-haired race. They called themselves 'the Cape people'. The other was a mixture of Hottentot, White, African and Bushman. These were flat-faced people, with tightly curled hair, who went by several names – for example the Griqua – but most proudly they went by the name of 'Bastards'.

It is against this background of enormous social upheaval that Christina and her family set out to find a farm, accompanied by the three children from her previous marriage. After trekking for about two months they came upon an abandoned farm that still had the remains of a house and stone kraal. They decided to stay.

The farm's name was Eseljacht and it was here that Christina bore three sons, Johannes, Coenraad and Frederick Petrus. In 1768, when Coenraad was seven, two brothers settled in the district and stocked their farm with cattle. They were David and Jacob Senekal. David was 29 and Jacob 27. Geertruy, Coenraad's favourite older sister, was 25 and wondering where she was going to find a husband. David Senekal provided the answer. The couple were married by a passing clergyman after six months together and Geertruy moved to the Senekal's farm.

Jacob remained a close friend of the Du Buis family and often visited the family home. One day, upon arrival, he discovered Jean sitting in a chair with his legs drawn up and stiff as planks. He was clutching his stomach and screaming. All that night he writhed in agony, watched over by his anxious family. The next day he was dead.

During that night Coenraad had walked to his sister's house to tell her the awful news. Geertruy was so shocked that she fainted. Upon recovering she told her young brother that she had seen another man die in exactly the same agonising way – her father, Christina's first husband. It was widely believed he had been poisoned. Coenraad decided never to return home again. Instead, he remained with Geertruy and her husband David on their farm. Coenraad's share of his father's estate allowed him to buy two cows and a dozen sheep, which he ran on his brother-in-law's farm. In time, the animals bred and his herd increased.

Six months later, Christina married Jacob Senekal. She was 48 years of age and Jacob 28. Within a few months Christina and Jacob, with all the children except Coenraad, trekked away.

At 11, Coenraad was taller than his brother-in-law; by the age of 13 he was over 6 ft. David did not like Coenraad, maybe because his size reduced David's authority, or maybe it was down to the fact that Coenraad was very polite and even-tempered. David disliked the way Coenraad had such a good rapport with the servants on the farm – they would do anything for Coenraad but remained surly towards him.

And so it came about that Coenraad, when he turned 18, went to live in a shack of his own on the farm. The farm prospered and so did Coenraad but the deep resentment David felt continued to fester. Over the years family tensions grew, leading to a final, decisive confrontation.

Geertruy visited Coenraad one day. Walking into the house, she saw Maria, her children's Hottentot nurse, sitting on the bed beside Coenraad. Coenraad rose in respect, Maria remained seated. 'Get up!' cried Geertruy. Maria rose. It was then that Geertruy noticed Maria's protruding stomach. Maria did not look perturbed; she even looked mildly amused. Geertruy was dumbfounded. There was no need to tell Coenraad to leave the farm, his demeanour told her that he was on his way.

'I have been hearing from my brother,' Conrad said. 'Now that the Xhosa have left the area between the Bushman and the Great Fish rivers, we will go and settle there. Maria has come to help me pack. By the way, you will need somebody else to tend the children, we shall be leaving tomorrow.'

In the area between the Bushman and the Great Fish Rivers, Coenraad and his brother Johannes were each granted the usual 6 000 acres of ground for 24 rix dollars per year. Then Petrus de Buys, their uncle, arrived and was allocated land beside theirs.

The Xhosa chief Langa (meaning 'day' or 'light') had moved to the eastern side of the Great Fish River. His tribe, the Amambala, would constantly come over the river and raid cattle, saying that the land was theirs and asking why they should not enjoy some of the fruits thereof. He was right. In 1779, by arbitrary decree, the Xhosa had been moved further eastwards – away from the lands they'd enjoyed possession of – and watched as the white settlers took over.

Archaeological evidence of pottery and other artefacts shows occupation of this area dating back to the seventh and eighth centuries. So much for the much-vaunted myth 'that nobody was there', it is just that – a myth. Systematically displaced from their ancestral grazing lands to make way for the new colonists and killed if daring to resist, the Xhosa, as with other disenfranchised tribes, were an angry, resentful people.

Coenraad's position was better, though he still had justifiable grievances. Cheap cattle farming was all very well, but the government did not, and could not, offer any form of security. So what, exactly, were he and the other settlers paying money for each year? Secondly, it was strictly against the law for the whites to cross the Fish River to retrieve cattle that had strayed there. Both sides felt aggrieved.

Coenraad, on his part, reasoned, 'The world does not always go as it should, it goes as it goes.' And, in the following dry season, he crossed the Fish River and brought cattle back from the Amambala tribe. In response, Langa's men invaded Coenraad's land and stole cattle in return. The two sides continued in this manner until, on one occasion, Coenraad came across a Xhosa making off with one of his prize cows and beat him.

Langa went to the authorities at Graaff-Reinet and stated that he was not intimidated and that, if this persisted, he would wage war against the Christians. The authorities went to see De Buys and asked whether he had crossed the border to raid cattle. 'Yes,' he replied, 'the government does not help us in any way so we have to help ourselves!'

Langa also charged De Buys with stealing one of his wives and two women from his captains. Coenraad admitted the charge but added that the captains' wives had returned. He also maintained that Langa's new young wife, Nomente, was happy to remain since the chief was a man of 80! Langa, in full force, invaded, killing people, burning houses, including De Buys's, and taking cattle as booty. And this is how the series of nine Frontier Wars, which was to mar our country for over a hundred years, began.

The Battle of Boomplaats

Let us revisit the Battle of Boomplaats, just to reiterate yet another example of the underlying British attitude towards South Africa during that time. The story centres on the infamous Harry Smith and specifically his lack of judgement and poor decision-making – flaws which undermined the time he spent in our country.

At the beginning of 1848 Harry Smith succeeded Sir Henry Pottinger as Governor of the Cape. His attitude hadn't matured nor changed at all from the time he had previously spent in the Eastern Cape. He saw it as his God-given task to, and I quote, 'bring under British control the numerous squabbling groups north of the Orange River'. He was of course referring to the Boers, the Griqua, the Baralong, the Batlokwa and the Basuthu. Some of these groups, such as the Griquas and the Basuthu, immediately saw the advantage of falling under the protection of the British, as this would place them in much stronger position when attempting to secure local 'bragging rights'.

The Boers, by contrast, had been forced to abandon their much loved Republic of Natalia because of British intervention. Knowing full well what British colonial expansion meant they were therefore in no mood for this self-opinionated Governor of the Cape. Smith suffered from delusions of grandeur – he actually believed that he was popular amongst the Boers and that the force of his personality would carry the day and settle matters decisively. So, in January 1848, he visited both Bloemfontein and Winburg where he received a cool but polite welcome. He then presented his case to his superiors in London, saying that the Boer population supported Britain taking over the land north of the Orange River.

On 3 February 1848, the theatrical Governor, on the banks of the Tugela River in Natal, issued a proclamation declaring the Queen's sovereignty over the whole area between the Orange and Vaal rivers, eastwards to the Drakensburg Mountains, waving away the concerns of Major Warden, the British Resident living in Bloemfontein (the town of Warden is named after him). Warden's concerns about security are dismissed by Smith who told him, 'The Boers are my children.' He then hurried away, leaving Warren with only a small number of Cape Mounted Rifles to look after this vast, turbulent territory.

The Boer leader, Pretorius, was having none of this. He rallied the majority of the Boers behind him and advanced on Bloemfontein. The commando of over 1 000 men was made up of 200 from the Transvaal and 800 from the Orange Free State. Major Warden had 57 troops from the Cape Mounted Rifles and 40 armed civilians. Of course, he had no option but to agree to the Boers' terms, which permitted him to withdraw southwards to the Cape with his personal belongings. On 20 July, the victorious Pretorius entered Bloemfontein. Just prior to this, on 13 July, Warden managed to get off a dispatch to Smith and the Governor wasted no time in responding, sending all available units to Colesburg.

The Orange River was in flood but Smith had brought with him two rubber floats. He crossed, with his entire army, at Botha's Drift. This took a full five days. Smith then drove his sizeable army, well over 1 000 men, along the Bloemfontein road to Vissershoek. He quite rightly expected Pretorius to defend the strongest position along this road, which was a group of hills some 25 km north of Vissershoek, centred on the farm called Boomplaats. Pretorius had done exactly that. The Boer outlying scouts reported Smith's imminent arrival and Pretorius lay in ambush.

The interesting fact about this battle is that Smith did not want to fight it. How could he, when it was he who had sold the idea of colonisation to his superiors in London (under the ruse that the Boers loved him so dearly), and yet here he had to stand and face them in battle? This could hardly have endeared him to his superiors. I have no doubt that Major Warden probably took most of the blame!

Although British losses were heavy their victory was, nevertheless, decisive and Smith marched into Bloemfontein. However, if you remember that it was only five years later that the British withdrew completely from what they termed the 'Orange River Sovereignty', you appreciate the very limited view Sir Harry Smith's foresight presented.

The Battle of Khunwana

I have come across a wonderful book which has recently been published. It is titled *Battles of South Africa* and the author is Tim Couzens. The book is a truly enthralling collection describing various battles between 1725 and 1927. What pleases me most is not only the wonderful research he has done, but also the fact that he actually tells you how to get there, what you will find, and of course the history around the incident. Wonderful stuff for people who have a love for our country and also for interested tourists.

One of his stories is called 'The Battle of Khunwana', which I would like to relate here.

It is the winter of 1832. Mzilikazi, the Ndebele king, is furious. He suspects the Tshidi Baralong of complicity with the Griqua in a recent cattle raid. 'Destroy Khunwana!' he cries.

If you look on a map, you will find Khunwana a couple of kilometres south of Kraaipan, the place where the first shots of the Anglo-Boer War were fired. There is virtually nothing there today; it is just a barren dust hole on the edge of the Kalahari Desert bereft of trees and with very little scrub bush. But, early one winter morning back in 1832, two royal scouts saw the dust rising from the running feet of the Ndebele warriors. There were thousands. They had run from Mosega, just north-east of Mafeking (now Mafikeng) with one purpose in mind: to raze Khunwana to the ground.

The Baralong scouts cried, 'Old guards and fresh conscripts – to the

Kgotla immediately, by command of the King!' and the men grabbed their assegais and shields. They were barely assembled before the Ndebele regiments were upon them, screaming the dreaded war cry – '*Mzilikaziiiii* ...' – and, with strange high-pitched hisses, they fell upon the Baralong warriors.

The Tshidi Baralong men fought hard – for their tribal pride, their wives and children, but most of all for their lives. The battle pattern was familiar and was known as 'The Horns of the Buffalo'. The two horns of the Ndebele, one led by Gobuza, the other by Gundwana, crushed the Baralong who turned and fled, knowing the battle was lost.

The Ndebele usually incorporated the vanquished tribes into their own, but not this time. The slaughter was furious and indiscriminate. Men, women and children were butchered as they ran in terror. Khunwana collapsed under flame and a large number of the royal family were killed. Survivors fled south to their cousins at Motlhanapitsi, near the present-day town of Warrenton.

The Tshidi Baralong, based near Warrenton, became uneasy when Mzilikazi moved dangerously close to their new position. So in 1833 they decided to move eastwards, to the black mountain called Thaba'Nchu. It was there that they met up with the voortrekkers and supported them after the Battle of Vegkop. Although the voortrekkers won that battle, they lost all their oxen and cattle to the Ndebele and it was the Baralong and the Basuto that supplied them with new animals.

Then, in the Battle of Mosega in 1837, the Baralong fought alongside the voortrekkers in their defeat of Mzilikazi, so avenging themselves of the destruction he had wreaked upon them five years earlier.

Penduka safaris

Cecil Barnard was a renowned elephant poacher, known by the local tribal people of the Mozambique bush as 'Bvenkenya'. His 'patch' was Crook's Corner in what is now familiar to us as the Kruger National Park. I had the honour of meeting his son, Izak, at the family farm near Geysdorp in the far North West district.

The area has quietness about it as only the distant North West has. There, on the farm, lies the grave of Bvenkenya. He died at home on 2 June 1962. When I say he was a poacher, I need to explain. Bvenkenya shot about one elephant per month and all the meat and skin would go to the tribe's people. Even today, the tribe will not grant a hunting concession to anybody else and the elders teach the young that this is Bvenkenya's land and that he will return. When Izak made a trip to his father's old stamping ground and got out of his Land Rover, the children shouted, 'Look! Bvenkenya has returned!' – such are the fond memories of these remote people.

This is Izak's tale of what the trip meant to him.

'Bvenkenya passed away and we put him away under the thorn trees. When the Diederik cuckoo came back with his very sad voice and the acacia trees had yellow flowers in their hair, I felt I had to go back to Crook's Corner. I sat there on the banks of the Levubu River and looked over it to Crook's Corner; to the big trees where the old adventurers had their camps, and to where the bush is secret and ageless.

'I dreamed away, and it was not long before I could see the dark figures sitting around the campfire. I could hear their yarns and laughter, hear stories of adventure and of the hunt; I could even see the dogs sitting on their haunches around the fire. It was then that I knew that Bvenkenya's spirit had wandered back to Crook's Corner, to join his wild companions of long ago, all of them following 'The Ivory Trail'.

'Gone forever are the old adventurers with their wonderful black companions who followed their masters on foot, many times leading them through paths unknown to white people, unveiling secrets of the old African bush. I could see the hunt. They would check the dung of the elephants first. You see, an elephant has six sets of teeth during the course of its life. When the elephant's last set starts to wear down, it can no longer chew properly. Because of this, the beast's digestive system alters and its dung becomes coarser and coarser – the coarser the dung, the older the elephant. These were the old bulls (with the biggest tusks) they used to cull.

'These were the people that found a silent grave in the African bush of long ago. My father had spoken to me that day. I headed back to the farm, to set up what is now the oldest safari company in Southern Africa. It is called 'Penduka', which means, "To turn around".'

Izak then told me more about farm life during his father's time. In the 1950s, the people from Tanganyika who had no money or jobs would walk all along the railway line to South Africa. At a place called Madibogo, they would leave the track and head eastwards right past the Barnards' farm. There they would stop and be given pap and bread with a cup of coffee. The next day they would continue their journey towards Klerksdorp to seek jobs in the mines. These people would walk for three months before arriving on the farm, and as the Barnards knew what hardship was, not one person would pass that farm gate without something to eat and drink. The people called him *'Bwana Nkuba'* – 'The good man with the deep heart'. Such was the mettle of those old farmers, and their rules of conduct and decency stand to this day.

When he was younger, Izak had to ride a bicycle to school in Klerksdorp – a distance of 160 km. He would then return home the same way at the end of term. Unperturbed by the huge distances involved, Izak considered himself lucky to have a bicycle! After schooling he rode to Johannesburg to get a job; a journey that takes three and a half hours by car today!

He also related the story of a African man named Ben Sighole who worked on a farm in the Vryburg district. With the outbreak of the Anglo-Boer War, Sighole rounded up all the farm's livestock and trekked deep into the Kalahari. There he stayed for three years. The family were disgusted with him – they thought he had stolen all the livestock. Then the English arrived. They shot all the remaining livestock in the entire area, burnt the farms and loaded the women and children into cattle trucks for transportation to the concentration camps. Ben Sighole stayed in the desert until the war ended then trekked back to the farm, livestock intact. His family were fortunate, since few people had anything left after the English departed. Such was the family's deep gratitude towards Ben that they presented him with half the farm. His descendants farm there to this day.

These are the stories our peoples need to know. As I have always said: there are more things in this country of ours that bind us together than keep us apart.

The Elephant House

Many of the old roads in South Africa were laid out along existing elephant trails. The Elephant House in Durban is sited on one of these ancient highways. It was built in the early 1850s on the highest natural point of the Berea Ridge, overlooking what is now called Jameson Park. At that time, the townlands of Durban included dense sub-tropical bush, mainly on the eastern slope of the Berea overlooking the bay and the Indian Ocean. To the west lay the farms – Cato Manor, Brickfields and Springfield. The dividing line between townlands and farmlands, which was surveyed and cut by the Forty Fifth Regiment, is now a combination of South Ridge Road, Ridge Road and North Ridge Road. The Elephant House was built on a portion of Springfield Farm, on the very edge of the townlands, and is the oldest surviving home in Durban.

The first landowner of this site was a trekker, Johannes Petrus Muller, who gained the land as a survey grant. The land was next transferred to the Milner Brothers in October 1847. Milner's Flagstaff was a well-known landmark on top of the Berea, indicating a footpath up the hill – today called Montpelier Road. The central section of the present house was built at this time. The Milners used the house as a hunting lodge and as a weekend retreat: an ideal alternative to the swampy and sandy townlands next to the bay. Today, if you stand on Ridge Road and close your eyes, you can picture the small community huddled around the bay and people hunting on the Berea.

In 1853 the house was sold to the Goodrickes. Four years later, it became the property of Edward Snell; then in 1863 it was bought by William Field, of Field Street fame. In 1883, Field sold it to Alexander

Murchie. It remained in that family until the present owner, Brian Agar, bought it in 1975.

The latest owners were going to tear the dilapidated building down, since it was on such a prime site, and start again from scratch. But, after lengthy debate, the family decided instead to renovate and maintain it for posterity. What a great decision – because this house was positioned right upon the elephants' migration trail! (It should be noted that the cost of refurbishing the home actually exceeded the original building costs.)

If you stand on the Ridge and look to your left, the area you see below you used to be a thick swamp forest: the natural habitat of the elephants that made their annual trek from the St Lucia district to the Zululand coast during the summer months. The house is situated directly on this route. As all old houses of that time, this one had a veranda or *stoep* all the way around it. This *stoep* was held up by solid Oregon pine pillars. The beasts, who did not tolerate humans kindly at all, used to brush up against the pillars, dislodging them from their bases!

During the renovation period many interesting items were unearthed, such as an old, green, square-faced bottle, which had held gin known as 'Genever' or 'Holland's' gin. All these artefacts have been preserved thanks to the efforts of the Agar family. One last interesting piece of information is the fact that immediately prior to the house being bought by the Agar family, a cannon from the wreck of the pepper ship *Aristo* had been donated by the Murchie family to the Old Fort Museum. The Agars, after the house was declared a national monument, asked for the cannon to be returned, which it was.

So, whenever you are in Durban and want to see a place of real interest just phone the Agar family; they will happily accept visitors by appointment. How nice it is to have people of that calibre in our midst. And the strange thing is that the house the elephants detested so much has, in fact, become the place that holds their memory today.

Forgotten tribes of the Gatsrand

On the southern side of the city of Johannesburg, disappearing in a westerly direction then curving slightly southwards, lies a range of hills known as the Gatsrand. There are portions of that range that are dolomitic in structure, which explains the name. Dolomite dissolves in water and the rains, falling through the atmosphere, pick up minute amounts of carbon dioxide. This in turn forms a weak solution of carbolic acid which, over millions of years, creates huge underground caverns. Hence the word *gat*, Afrikaans for hole.

As the range stretches westwards and just after the little mining town of Carletonville, there lies one of the original springs of the Mooi or, to give it its ancient black name, Tlokwe River. It's a beautiful place where the crystal clear waters flow gently by. Tom and Day Coulter have owned this magnificent spot of paradise for over 50 years and it is here that they raised their family. The old pre-Boer home they live in was original home to the famous Piet Bezuidenhout of Potchefstroom, the one who would not pay the tax on his gunpowder: an event that was one of causes of the First Anglo-Boer War of 1880–81. It is to Tom and Day that I'm indebted for the wonderful tale that follows.

It was in 1934 that the Reverend R Patterson, visiting parishioners, first heard of a large and unusual cave in the area. He took a brief look but realised that without a ladder he was unable to enter the cave. Patterson returned home and mentioned his discovery to a friend, Brumage, who was interested in everything archaeological. The pair organised an exploratory party which included Dr Friel, Leonard Brown and a retired magistrate, Mr F Lawrence. Upon entering the cave the men found circular huts of about a metre and a half in diameter. They were all made of stone and daub and had no roofs.

Six years later Brumage led another party, this time with heavyweights involved: Dr Basil Cooke, geologist, Miss E Haughton from the Transvaal Museum, and Dr H Wells, later to become the Professor of Anatomy at the University of Cape Town.

Around the entrance to the cave they found ruins of fairly typical southern Transvaal Iron Age settlements. The cave entrance led down over stony debris (called talus), into a large central vault some 10 to 12 metres below ground level. The average height of the cave was about two metres. There were several secondary chambers, some narrow and low, others wider, with domed roofs.

As the party explored the complex, they found several rusted iron implements, as well as weapons. One such find was a battle-axe, the wooden haft still attached to the axe. They bent down to retrieve it but the haft turned to dust upon being touched. (Incidentally, Leonard Brown was reputed to have a fine collection of some half dozen spearheads and axes, collected from the ledges in the rock walls of the Gatsrand cave.) Other finds by that first expedition included the incomplete model of an ox, and two blackened, carved, wooden tinderboxes. There were also several human bones, which, I'm sorry to say, also crumbled when touched.

The local peoples told Brumage that they were descendants of the people in the cave, and that between 1820 and 1830 their ancestors had taken refuge there. During that time, Mzilikazi's warriors were laying waste the entire countryside, from the Limpopo in the north to the Lekoa, or Vaal, in the south. They informed Brumage that there were two tribes who had particular past associations with the cave – the Kwena and the Phiring.

The Kwena, now living in the Rustenberg or Thalabeng area (Thalabeng meaning 'The Place of Stabbing'), told the government ethnologist Dr P H Brentz that their forefathers had entered the Transvaal under a chief named Maselwane. Mzilikazi tried in vain to capture Maselwane, who fled southwards to the Gatsrand, where he took refuge in the cave.

Maselwane and his tribe built a stone ramp into the cave and then led all the women, children and cattle down. The stones were then moved to another part of the cave. This meant that if anyone wanted to enter they would have to jump down to the floor far below, where they would be immediately set upon. When it was safe to leave, the ramp would be re-laid and the stronghold exited. And, in a remote recess of the cave was grass matting stuck into a fissure in the rock – remove it and fresh water flowed. What a fortress!

Maselwane then attacked one of Mzilikazi's impis, stealing his cattle. Mzilikazi chased him into the Free State where he met up with the voortrekker Hendrik Potgieter. The voortrekkers gave him the name Selon – hence the Selons River in the Madikwi district of the North West Province. It was Maselwane who showed the voortrekkers the whereabouts of Mzilikazi's stronghold at Mosega, where the chief was defeated and put to flight.

When Mzilikazi fled he took the Phiring tribe north with him. The tribe, however, deserted. In 1837 the Phiring, arriving at Lepolang, found the Gatsrand cave occupied by the Kwena. Mabelane, the Phiring chief, was permitted to shelter his people in the cave, though later they moved to the Lamane Hills in the Potchefstroom region.

This marvellous cave is still there and can be visited through contacting the Trans-Vaal Branch of the Archaeological Society.

The baboon of Uitenhage

In the early 1890s, in the little town of Uitenhage in the Eastern Cape, lived a man by the name of James Wide. Mr Wide worked as a signalman for South African Railways at the Uitenhage terminus. Tragically, he was involved in a terrible railway accident that resulted in both his legs being amputated at the knee. But our Mr Wide had an indomitable spirit and no little ingenuity: he decided to train a baboon to assist him in his work as a signalman!

The baboon's name was Jack. First, Jack was taught how to take out the little railway scotch car, place it on the rails, then push Mr Wide up the tracks to check the points. That done, Jack would learn that he must push his instructor back to the terminus. Jack was then trained, by verbal command, which of the railway track levers to pull down and which to lift up. And so Jack's training as a signalman's assistant progressed. It is recorded that this faithful creature completed his tasks perfectly for over 10 years! (I wonder if that was not the origin of 'Task analysis' in South Africa!)

It was a sad day when, on 15 April 1890, Jack the baboon signalman died. And just in case anybody doubts the validity of this lovely story, I quote an excerpt from a letter written by a Mr H W Bidwell to Dr Selma Schöland, the then Director of the Albany Museum:

'I have succeeded in getting a promise from Mr Wide here to send you the skin etc. of the most distinguished baboon that the world knows about. His fame has been publicised all over the world. I think that the animal would be of great attraction to your Museum.'

There also survives a letter from Mr Wide himself to Dr Schöland, stating that he would have much pleasure in forwarding the skin and also a pair of photographs showing Jack at work. I have copies of these two unbelievable photographs. James Wide asks, most touchingly, that, 'I wish him to be mounted sitting in a chair with his left hand resting on his knee, as that was a favourite position of his when he was alive.'

Unfortunately, Mr Wide's wish could not be fulfilled. A note written on the back of this letter, in Dr Schöland's handwriting and bearing his initials, said this: 'The skin was sent back the same day as it was in very bad condition.' Alas, too, Jack's skull cannot be singled out in the Albany Museum as a sizeable collection of baboon skulls is housed there.

Sir Harry Smith

Sir Harry Smith and his darling wife, Juana Maria de los Delores de Leon, are the people that both Harrismith and Ladysmith in Natal are named after. Other towns in our country that carry associations with them are Mossel Bay, which was originally called Aliwal South, and Aliwal North, that well-known hot-spring spa. The name Aliwal comes from Sir Harry's victory over the Sikhs during the British wars in India. Another town, Juanasberg in the Amatolas, was named after Smith's wife. Now, however, it lies deserted, burnt to the ground during the Frontier Wars of the Eastern Cape.

Juana Maria de los Dolores de Leon was the orphaned child of an old aristocratic Spanish family, and she was raised in a convent school in the city of Badajos, Spain. By the time she was 14 she had lived through two sieges and celebrated her birthday during a third. Young as she was, she had already held her wounded and dying brother in her arms. She had seen the streets of her native city being occupied by Spanish, French and British troops.

Just after the Battle of Talavera, when Juana was 11 years old, Lord Wellington had made Badajos his headquarters and Lord Fitzroy Somerset had been billeted in the house of Juana's elder sister, whose husband was a Spanish officer. Fitzroy Somerset, afterwards Lord Raglan, Commander in Chief of the Crimea, was a man of impeccable and noble character and the impression that he made upon little Juana de Leon was to last the rest of her life.

Just before Juana's fourteenth birthday, Badajos belonged to the French and was cut off from the outside world. On 17 March 1812, Lord Wellington laid siege to the city and breached the walls with his artillery.

The defending officers knew then that they had reached 'the last moment' – the critical point when a decision had to be made either to surrender or continue defending the city. Surrender would ensure the survival of the inhabitants; defending it would invite death and destruction – the town would be looted, the streets swarming with men excited by victory and maddened by liquor.

Phillipon, the gallant Commandant of the French troops, was not about to bow to Wellington, and what followed has forever been a blight upon British military history.

Even Lord Napier, who later became the Governor of the Cape, penned bitter words regarding the scenes that followed:

'Now commenced that wild and desperate wickedness, which so tarnished the lustre of the soldiers' heroism, shameless rapacity, brutal intemperance, savage lust, cruelty, murder, piteous lamentations, the hissing of the burning houses, the crashing of doors and windows, the rapports of muskets being used in violence resounded for two days and nights in the streets of Badajos.'

Juana's eldest sister, Senora, lived in the aristocratic quarter, and in that saturnalian drinking plunder her house was ransacked. The two girls ran to Fitzroy Somerset and begged for mercy and protection, which they were afforded. Somerset was smitten by the younger sister's sheer beauty, but it was his more impudent fellow and friend, one Harry Smith of the same regiment, who stole the day.

Lieutenant-Colonel Henry George Wakelyn Smith, later known as Lieutenant-General Sir Harry Smith, Baronet of Aliwal – dashing, vain, self-glorifying, reckless, somewhat mad and often ludicrous, was someone you never forgot. Born the fifth of 11 children to a country surgeon in 1787, Harry joined the Yeoman Calvary, aged 16. In 1805 he was gazetted as a Second Lieutenant in the Green Jackets of the 95th Regiment of Riflemen – 'The Rifle Brigade' as they became known.

Smith was a dashing blade, a fine soldier and, when he met Juana, a Brigade Major in the Light Division. Warm hearted and generous, the 22-year-old Harry swept the young Spanish maiden off her feet. Of courtship and wooing there was little to speak of: two days later, Lord

Wellington himself gave Juana Maria de los Dolores de Leon away to Harry Smith in marriage.

From that day forth it was 'follow the drum' for little Juanita. She accompanied her beloved 'Enree' through every battle, every hardship, every suffering and every euphoric victory. On many occasions she gave him up for dead, searching the battlefields amongst the victims, only to be relieved and delighted to find him alive. The officers and the troops of the British army grew to adore her, admiring her courage, her indomitable spirit and the ingenuous dedication she showed to her husband.

Smith sailed to South America, as the British sought to extend their hegemony there, only to fail miserably. Next, under Sir John Moore, he crossed the seas to Sweden in the company of 10 000 men. Having no idea what they should do when they arrived, the fleet lay at anchor off Gothenburg and never landed! In Spain, standing against Napoleon's invasion of Iberia, Smith's and his nation's involvement in the conflict ended in an infamous, disorderly retreat! They were evacuated back to England, only to return four months later, this time under the command of Sir Arthur Wellesley, later known as the Duke of Wellington – 'The Iron Duke'.

Every officer who attained Wellington's approbation and the friendship of his Military Secretary, Fitzroy Somerset, was always recommended for a plum job. The other officers, not so favoured by the command, were reduced to mean pickings during the harsh economic circumstances that followed war. Harry Smith was one of the favoured ones. Sent to the Cape as Quartermaster-General, for four years Smith kicked his heels under Sir Benjamin D'Urban, until his chance to shine finally arrived.

On December 28 1834 an exhausted horseman galloped into the Cape Town garrison carrying the news that the Xhosa had 'invaded' the Eastern Frontier. D'Urban instructed Smith to go and take charge of the situation immediately.

The normal route was to go up the coast by ship, but not for our hero – Smith decided to be an active traveller and ride there, as opposed to idling as a passenger on a supply ship. It took two days to lay on fresh horses for Smith along the way. As the ship sailed from Simon's Town,

Smith bid farewell to his beloved Juana and galloped off on the first leg of his 900 km ride to Grahamstown. This was showmanship at its best!

We must say a little about this so-called 'Xhosa interruption'. It was greeted in Cape Town with shocked disbelief. The Colony had taken Xhosa forbearance for granted; after all, the local peoples had been satisfactorily intimidated by the show of colonial power and were supposed to be happy with their lot! This arrogant complacency was so prevalent that not even the missionaries, who were closer than most to the Xhosa, saw trouble brewing. The hubris of the civil establishment in Grahamstown, the incompetence of military leaders, and the smugness of the settlers themselves – never deigning to take the Xhosa's views into consideration – was about to be severely tested.

The various Xhosa clans started to invade the frontier – the Rharhabe, Ngqika, Nlambes, Ngqeno, Galecka and Gqunukhwebe, although, at this stage, the Gqunukhwebe, Phato, Kama and Cebo Chungwa were not formally at war.

Picture the scene: the average Xhosa, having lost his grazing grounds to the invading white colonists, having been treated with disdain and displaced by the gun, now gets called upon to make a stand. Dressed in their regimental finery with feathers and plumes in their headbands, whipped up into an emotional frenzy by their chiefs and sangomas, smoked up into a haze of bloodlust, they descended upon the unsuspecting settlers to regain their lost lands. There was nothing that was going to stop them. Naked and masked in red clay, a beaded band adorned with Blue Crane feathers around their shaven heads, they were the exact opposite of the passive, amiable and pliable Xhosa that the missionaries had sought to convert.

The warriors had been told not to harm the missionaries, who, standing outside their various stations, watched in terror as wave after wave of warriors jogged past. There was exemption for no one else; only the missionaries were spared. One missionary, Gotlieb Kayser, was about to experience exactly what that meant. A trader named Warren had taken refuge in his mission. Maqoma's Ngqika came to the door and demanded that Warren come out. Kayser, crying and pleading for Warren's life, was told, 'Shut up and go into your house!' He was pushed inside. Then, the shout went up, 'These people have murdered enough of ours!' The terrified Warren was dragged away and cut to death on the front lawn.

In the absence of any form of organized resistance the Xhosa fell upon the settlers. Murder, theft, fire and total destruction spread almost as far as Uitenhage and Somerset East. This was the beginning of what is now being called South Africa's Hundred Years War.

It is worthwhile recalling that during this era the career advancements for military men relied on successful completions and conclusions of sorties, campaigns and warfare in general. The prospects for advancement without these being in place were pretty dismal. So, come what may, the ever ambitious Smith was going to get his fair share of glory out of what he called the Xhosa's defiance of British military might.

Let us first consider how he treated the local Boers. He regarded them with absolute distain and considered them to have no backbone or spunk whatsoever. In the many letters that he wrote to his beloved Juana in Cape Town, he shows this disdain time and time again. The way in which he describes the campaigning in British Kaffaria is best highlighted in another officer's own words – 'I do not think him to be a liar, but let us just say that he is an extremely bad witness.'

Smith had one of those personalities whereby he could only see what he thought should be the case and not the reality of the event. He talks about 'thoroughly thrashing the Xhosa warriors' and making them all flee from British Kaffaria, and of capturing thousands of head of cattle. But he and D'Urban actually realised that to push the Xhosa out of Albany and east of the Great Fish River was pointless. Having an arbitrary line to their own territory, the Xhosa merely stole cattle and retreated back over the river. If the British came after them the Xhosa objected, quite properly, that they were invading their land.

Smith, however, was not going to botch this one: his career depended upon it. Eventually he succeeded in convincing D'Urban that the Great Fish River, with its steep and wooded banks, was not a good place for territory marking. Rather, they should extend that boundary eastwards to the Great Kei River, about 100 km from the paramount chief of the

Xhosa's great kraal. This meant that the areas occupied by the Ngqeno, Botomane, Dushane and other minor chiefs were to be appropriated and the tribes pushed westwards to the other side of the Kei River. It never crossed the mind of this conceited, arrogant officer that he might be worsening and hardening the feelings of the Xhosa. Conversely, Smith felt they must be compelled to bow down before the imperial majesty of the British crown.

Smith had about 1 200 men – the Seventy Second Highlanders, the Seventy Fifth Regiment and the Albany Sharpshooters, as well as volunteer Burgers from Uitenhage, George and Graaff-Reinet. At this point, I'd like to quote from one of Smith's letters to Juana, dated 25 March 1835. Reading this, you can appreciate the nature of the man:

'A young, big, fat Dutchman has just come to my tent door saying that he has no blanket and that he is very wet, what is he to do? – Go to the Devil and warm yourself you spoony. Make a fire, sir, and sing over it. I have given you grog – why, I never had a blanket, campaigning for 10 years. What you require sir is pluck. Now be off with you!'

Hardly the way to treat men who have volunteered. But such was the conceit of the man that he said the local Boers loved him dearly. He also had no doubt that, on his return trip to Cape Town, the townsfolk would come out in their droves to welcome him as he rode through.

The Xhosa never actually left Albany and British Kaffraria; they merely retired to the thicker bush and hid. It was then that Smith convinced Hintsa, the chief of the Gqunukhwebe, to come and discuss the possibility of peace and an amnesty. However, over a period of weeks, Hintsa found his status changing from that of a visiting foreign sovereign to that of a fugitive captive. Smith constantly harangued him, demanding that all the Xhosa lay down their assegais and, as a penalty, pay a fine of 50 000 cattle and 1 000 horses. I don't think that I'm alone in finding this an extremely high price for people to pay an invader of their own territory.

The history books tell us that it was Hintsa's idea for Smith and a group of his men to accompany him back to his great place to collect all the cattle. Reading between the lines, it is clear that this was probably

Smith's idea. In any event, a party with Smith and Hintsa in it set off. In the vicinity of Butterworth, half the group stopped, exhausted. Smith left them behind and rode on.

The remaining group had climbed a steep hill when, at its summit, Hintsa broke into a full gallop. Smith gave chase. Being the lighter man and having a horse in better condition, Smith soon came within firing range, only for both pistols to misfire. They careered on. Smith spurred his horse alongside and managed to unsaddle Hintsa, who then broke free and ran for the wooded banks of the Nqabara River. George Southey, a member of Smith's party, called twice in Xhosa for Hintsa to stop. Southey then fired and hit the chief in the leg, although this did not stop him. Southey fired again and hit Hintsa in the back. The chief plunged down the steep river bank to seek shelter. There, Southey came upon him and, ignoring his pleas for mercy, blew his brains out at point blank range.

With the killing of the leading chief of the Xhosa people, did the colonists really think that this would be the end? It proved to be just the beginning.

If one reads A L Harrington's account of Harry Smith's time in South Africa, it is no wonder he subtitled the book, *Bungling Hero*. As Harrington traces Smith's 15 years in South Africa, firstly at the centre of complex and controversial affairs of the Eastern Cape, then as Governor and High Commissioner of the Cape of Good Hope, it becomes apparent that he made as many bad decisions as good. I do not, personally, think highly of the man. However, let me hasten to add that I judge him through today's eyes, and as we know hindsight has the benefit of 20-20 vision. And, Smith's roll-call of engagements as an active soldier is impressive: Montevideo, Corunna, Busaco, Fuentes d'Onor, Ciudad Rodrigo, Badajos, Salamanca, Vittorio, Pyrenees, Nivelle, Nive, Orthez, Toulouse, Peninsular, Bladensburg and Waterloo, not to mention the Frontier Wars or the Indian campaigns. This grand old soldier, for all his mistakes, is still worthy of our respect.

One thing that cannot be questioned is the undying love he had for his wife. He passed away on 12 October 1860, aged 74; Juana continued to sing his praises after he was gone. She died 12 years later almost to the day, on 10 October 1872. The couple rest, side by side, in the cemetery at Whittlesea in Britain (where the town of the same name in the Eastern Cape gets its name from).

So, when next you travel through places like Harrismith, Ladysmith or Whittlesea, spare a thought for that brave Spanish girl and the soldier who adored her all his life.

The *Alabama*

Like so many other children of my time, I got to know the old Cape Malay song, 'Daar kom die Alabama'. And, like so many other things these days, the story attached to this song is beginning to slip away and become lost in the mists of time. Let me put that right ...

The *Alabama* was built in Birkenhead in Britain and launched there on 24 August 1862. She was a warship of 1 000 tons, used by the Confederate States of America during the Civil War of 1861–65. They used her as a raider, targeting the trading ships of the North. The story of how she ended up in our waters and what happened when she did is fascinating.

She had been zigzagging through the South Atlantic between Brazil and the west coast of Africa, when on 28 July 1863 the ship's commander, one Captain Raphael Semmes, decided, for fear of running into Northern warships to put in at Saldanha Bay. He wrote in his diary that he found it very strange that everyone had chosen to settle in Cape Town. Saldanha, in his view, had much better anchorage and was completely protected from the windy gales that beset the Cape. It was also spacious enough to accommodate the largest of fleets. 'There is no finer sheet of water than this in the world,' he wrote.

Semmes sent his paymaster ashore to buy fresh provisions, as well as travel south to inform the Governor of the Cape, Sir Philip Wodehouse, of his arrival. The paymaster secured some excellent venison from the local Dutch farmers. This pleased the crew greatly as it made a welcome change from the salted-meat diet of life at sea. Some of the men were allowed ashore to go rabbit and bird shooting.

During the week the *Alabama* remained, local farmers were invited aboard for a tour of the ship. After all, she was well known, and her success in raiding a large number of ships belonging to the North was common knowledge. The role she played had, of course, aroused different feelings on both sides of the Atlantic. Despite the fact that slavery was unpopular in Britain, the Confederates were nevertheless regarded as romantic fighters by many. President Abraham Lincoln's government was, by contrast, not best pleased to learn that the *Alabama* had been built and equipped as a raider in Britain. This was made very clear in a letter of protest lodged with Sir Philip Wodehouse. Wodehouse answered, rather smartly, by saying that the British government was neutral and that as the ship had put in to Saldanha for repairs and he had received no instructions to impound her, she would complete her painting before going on her way.

Painting finished, the *Alabama* sailed into Table Bay on 5 August 1863, accompanied by her supply ship, the *Tuscaloosa*. The event that followed was to cement the ship's fame in our country's naval history.

They were hauling in for Cape Town, just after noon, when a sail was spotted from the crow's nest, identified as a newly painted American barque. The wind was light and the barque was not making much headway. This was unfortunate, for if she could have made the charmed 'Marine League', that is, territorial waters, she would have been safe. The *Alabama*'s engineers piled every ounce of steam into the boilers, and, firing cannon across her bows, made the barque heave to.

It is now many years later, but to read the old *Cape Argus* account of the taking of the vessel still makes your hair rise. The paper describes how the entire city came to a standstill, intrigued by the drama unfolding in the bay. All the city cabs were hired as people swarmed up Lion's Hill to Kloof Road for a better view. Here's what one eye witness said:

'As soon as we reached the crown of the hill, we set off at breakneck pace, down the hill, past the Round House, till we came near Brighton, and there lay the *Alabama*, within 50 yds of the unfortunate Yankee. The weather was calm, and the sea like glass. The barque was making her way slowly from the steamer, with every bit of her canvas spread, and the *Alabama*, with her steam off, seemed to be letting the barque get away.'

The barque wasn't escaping. Because, like a cat playing with a mouse, Captain Semmes let his prize draw off before he pounced. Slowly, the *Alabama* sailed around the *Sea Bride* (the fated vessel's name) and closed to within 20 yards of the ship. A boat was lowered and the crew took possession of the vessel. Within minutes, the *Sea Bride* was disappearing over the horizon. The *Alabama* sailed into Cape Town, the streets lined with people to welcome her. No matter the political context of what had just occurred, the people's hearts and imaginations had been touched by what they had witnessed and the *Alabama* was feted like a hero.

Messrs Searight & Co called upon Captain Semmes and offered to purchase the *Sea Bride*. A deal was struck and the vessel handed over at a remote place called Angra Pequena, today known as Lüderitz Bay.

The North, understandably, did not take this defeat lying down and sent the warship *Vanderbilt* to the Cape. It was, apparently, quite a sight to see how the *Alabama* managed each time to evade the *Vanderbilt* before setting sail for the Brazilian coast. A while later the *Alabama* returned to the Cape, still a hero in the eyes of the people. She then made the long voyage back across the equator and, eventually, docked at the French port of Cherbourg. It was here where fate overtook her: the Union government had sent the armour-plated *Kearsage* to deal with her.

On 19 June 1864, with thousands of French citizens watching the battle, the *Alabama* was hit, then sank beneath the waves. There were many sad hearts in Cape Town when the news of her demise arrived. In 1890, an old sailor passed away in Mossel Bay. His name was John Moore – the gunner on the *Kearsage* who had fired the shot that sent the *Alabama* down.

Thankfully, she still lives on in our song.

Changes leading to chaos and conflict

Not many people are aware that the old town of Mafikeng (formerly Mafeking) in the North Western Province (formerly the Far Western Transvaal) has been besieged twice, and that the Anglo-Boer War blockade was the second of the two occasions. The first is the subject of this story.

The period from the late 1870s onwards was an extremely difficult time for all concerned in that part of our country. The discovery of diamond fields in 1867, then the founding of Kimberley in 1870, brought profound changes to the peoples of the region, many causing profound misery and hardship.

In 1871 the disputed territory was granted to the Griqua chief, Nikolaas Waterboer, instead of the Transvaal Republic, causing resentment and bitterness in the Boer community. At the same time, the local surrounding tribes are vying for a chunk of this new economic wealth. In and around the region are the Thlaping, the Rolong, the Tlharo and the Kora – the two main tribes being the Thlaping and the Rolong.

Montshiwa, the chief of the Rolong is established in Vleifontein (present day Rooigrond) in the Malopo area. Trouble starts when one Hans Coetzee begins to reap the chief's wheat crops for himself. This act precipitates the beginning of the so-called Bechuanaland Wars, after Montshiwa responds in force by deploying 3 000 troops to repel the invaders. It is not only white trespassers that Montshiwa has to contend with, but also competing Rolong tribes who have flooded into the newly prosperous area. These minor chiefs are keen to hire returning Boer mercenaries, fresh from their victory over the British in the First Anglo-Boer War of 1880–81.

In the south, the Thlaping experiences follow the same pattern – minor chiefs recruiting white mercenaries on the promise of land and cattle, if successful in battle.

From 1881 to 1884 it is estimated that Mankurwane, the Thlaping's chief, loses in excess of 50 000 cattle as he battles hostile takeovers of his grazing lands.

In 1877, Montshiwa confronts a crisis as two displaced chiefs from the Lotlhakane, Moswete and Matlabe, invade his principal town, Sehuba. The chiefs have the help of Gey van Pittius, Johannes Otto and another 200 mercenaries. The Rolong are driven out of Sehuba and seek refuge in Mafeking where they are besieged by their adversaries. In one month alone Montshiwa loses 5 000 cattle and 300 horses.

As the beleaguered Rolong run desperately low on food, Montshiwa pleads with the British to annex the territory and rid the land of these unwelcome intruders. His entreaty falls on deaf ears. His people starving and the supply lines to Kimberley under control of the fed and watered mercenaries, Montshiwa has no option but to capitulate.

The terms of his surrender are severe: relinquishment of all Rolong land south of the Malopo, destruction of all stone defence works in Mafeking and a massive fine. When Montshiwa refused to accept these terms, they simply forged his signature on the already prepared document.

The Limpopo Province

'The Limpopo Province: the undiscovered jewel of the North', I read on a billboard when driving through the area. What an understatement! I imagined myself standing in the southern lee, looking northwards to the mighty Zoutpansberg. Ahead and slightly to the left, I could see the wonderful hideaway resort of Buzzard Mountain, owned by John and Gail Greeves. Standing on their part of the mountain in the early morning, watching the black eagles soaring in the clear skies, you appreciate what a beautiful, restorative place it is.

The province affords the traveller many interesting sights and stories. For example, Schoemansdal: a ruined frontier town that used to be the ivory-trading capital of the North. Every year during the 1860s a fair was held in Schoemansdal and traders would come from the Cape, Natal and Portuguese East Africa to buy ivory. The market square would be filled with piles of huge, white tusks, taken from the thousands of elephants slaughtered each year. The Strubens, well known traders from Pretoria (Strubens Valley is named after them), would take about 32 000 pounds alone. As the average elephant carried approximately 200 pounds in ivory weight, 160 elephants per year would have been needed to satisfy their needs alone.

Ivory was also the cause of the ultimate destruction of Schoemansdal by the BaVenda chief Makhato. In the 1860s, Schoemansdal was divided over the distribution of wealth from ivory trading. Previously, the local peoples had acted as bearers, butchers, and guides. But lately the men of

Schoemansdal had become lazy. They'd given guns to the BaVenda, shown them the craft of elephant hunting and then sent then off to track down and kill these gentle giants. However, the Boers still expected to receive the major portion of the hunt spoils. Naturally, the elephant hunters were having none of this so they quit the village, taking the guns and tusks with them. When the return of both was demanded, they refused.

Makhato, the BaVenda chief, then decided to go to war. Schoemansdal was laagered – Paul Kruger, along with 400 men, rode up from Pretoria. Their efforts were destined to fail – the supply lines were too long, the night sky along the southern Zoutspansberg was peppered with the fires of the warring BaVenda and alarm calls were continuous throughout the night.

On 15 July 1867, Kruger gave the community three days to pack up and return south to Marabastad. It was with heavy hearts that they left. Looking back, they could see the smoke rising as the BaVenda razed their homes and their church to the ground.

The district, once a flourishing trading area, was now bankrupt, and the only one to remain was Juwawa Albasini, still stubbornly entrenched in his fortress some 40 km east of the ruined and deserted town. Makhato continued to wage war against the whites. An English ivory hunter, Haines, who persisted in his enterprise, had his throat cut. Two prospectors, Charles Muller and George Anderson, who were fossicking north of the Zoutspansberg, were attacked. Anderson and two of the servants had their throats cut; Muller escaped by creeping through the grass.

Makhato had won the day, and the endless wars ruined Albasini. On 10 July 1888 he died – a weary and disappointed man.

Nomansland

If you travel south along the N2 from Durban and leave the ocean behind you at Port Shepstone, you start climbing into the hills and mountains heading towards Kokstad. Just before Kokstad you get the beautiful Ingeli Forest, with the admirable Ingeli Forest Lodge. It is here, in this area of Mount Currie, Kokstad and Ingeli, that this story unfolds.

Adam Kok was a disillusioned man when he arrived in the area called Nomansland. The Griqua had been trekking for three years, all the way from Philippolis in the Cape, through Basutoland – blasting their path open at times with dynamite – to get away from the despised British who ruled in the Cape. Kok's people had formed their first laager on the slopes of Mount Currie, fortified with stacked sods of earth which dried like cement. They stayed there for nine years.

Adam Kok, wishing to improve the moral 'tone' of the community, had ridden to Cape Town to get a preacher. A Reverend William Dower had agreed to come, on condition that the people laid out a proper town for themselves. The preacher arrived at the laager in the autumn of 1869. Kok then hired the services of a land surveyor called Edward Barker to lay out the town. It was to be named Kokstad. He also asked Donald Strachan, a white trader, to become the town's first magistrate.

The new town was laid out in 1870. However, the people refused to move even though they were offered free residential stands. Instead, they stayed on in the fortified laager on the slopes of Mount Currie. Kok eventually lost his patience. He instructed his officials to move all the arms, ammunition and government property to the new town, and warned the citizens that, unless they moved immediately, they would be afforded no protection!

There was at this time an unfortunate incident that was used as an excuse by the British to interfere in the Griqua affairs. A commission from the Cape was sent to look at tribal boundaries, and in 1873 Joseph Orpen was appointed British Resident of the Transkei. Orpen did not like the Griquas and encouraged more white farmer settlers into the area, thus providing the British government with additional justification, bogus though it was, for annexation of the area.

The stage is now set for the arrival of a central character: an individual by the name of Smith Plommer. In his youth Plommer had served in the Cape Corps, but in 1850 he had joined the Kat River Rebellion. When the rebellion was suppressed he and 400 of his followers fled to Nomansland to live as outlaws. The British put a price on his head, dead or alive. To secure allies, it was Plommer who had ridden to Philippolis and persuaded the Griquas to come to Nomansland. And it was Smith Plommer who was the first to join the Griquas on Mount Currie, though most of their women and children (including Plommer's wife) had been killed in the Bhaca reprisal the year before.

Smith Plommer began plotting to overthrow Kok. He gave up transport riding between Natal and Kokstad and returned to cattle rustling along with Ludewyk and Muis Kok, keeping a close watch on local affairs.

In 1874 the British annexed Nomansland. The situation was hopeless. What could a few thousand ill-equipped irregulars do against the military might of the British Army? To cap it all, Adam Kok died after falling from his wagon and being ridden over. Now, there was no obvious successor to lead the Griqua.

To make matters worse, in 1876 Captain Blythe arrived with the Cape Mounted Rifles and was soon convinced that he had a rebellion on his hands. He searched all the houses and uncovered all manner of arms and ammunition. The Griqua mood grew more rebellious. Muis Kok travelled to Pondoland and convinced a chief, together with 94 of his men, to join the rebellion. When Smith Plommer heard of these developments he, with over 300 Xhosa, hurried to join Muis and together they raided farms for horses, guns and cattle.

Five hundred 'rebels' gathered at the deserted old fort on the slopes of

Mount Currie, having sent messages urging Blythe to attend a meeting between the two sides. Blythe was uninterested in debate and called instead for their immediate surrender. When they refused, Captain Blythe sent his personal carriage to the laager to remove Adam Kok's widow, for he did not want her involved in the fighting. He then gave the order to attack. The battle lasted barely four hours. Twelve Griquas, including Muis Kok, lay dead; the rest fled with Smith Plommer towards Pondoland – Smith still with a price on his head.

Fearing that the rebels might regroup, Blythe sent a detachment of mounted police under Donald Strachan to bring them in. They overtook the rebels on the slopes of the Ingeli Mountains and surrounded them. On 17 April 1878 Smith Plommer was counted amongst the 20 dead Griqua on the side of Ingeli Mountain. They slung Plommer's body over a horse and conveyed it to Kokstad, where the soldiers cut off his head before burying the body. The men claimed the reward, only to pass it on to a widow whose husband had been killed – blown up when the rebels ignited the town's powder magazine.

Thus ended the independence. Ironically enough, the name of East Griqualand only came into being *after* British annexation.

An ancient South African battle

The battle in question came to pass as the result of greed, as so many acts of warfare do. In this case, greed for gold – the legendary gold of Ophir (which King Solomon's men transported 420 talons of back to the Temples). The conflict took place in 1725 in an area of the country which is familiar to us as the lower region of the Kruger National Park.

The tale begins with a Johan Christofel Steffler, born in Magdaburg, Germany to a well-to-do trading family. After obtaining a first-class education, Johan became increasingly fascinated by his eldest brother's trading stories from Africa. Travel beckons and Johan, after securing a position with the Dutch East India Company, is shipped off to the Cape of Good Hope.

The Dutch have heard of the fabulously wealthy Ophir, an ancient site referred to in the Bible and are also intrigued by the local peoples' reverential talk of the treasure of Monomotapa, deep within the African interior.

Steffler and the other Dutch explorers head for a ruined settlement based around an old Portuguese fort, La Goa, in Delagoa Bay. The Portuguese had started a trading post there, only for that dream to disappear as the ubiquitous mosquito devastated the community. Vacated by these earlier settlers, the fort had fallen into a state of disrepair.

On 29 March 1720 three Dutch ships – the *Kaap*, *Gouda* and *Zeelandia* are cordially welcomed by the local tribe, the Batonga and

Chief Maphumbo. The ships carry craftsmen, sailors and soldiers, and all set about fortifying the old structure. Within three weeks, however, over 100 of them have died of fever. In August of the same year 80 replacements arrive.

The improved fort is called Fort Lydsaamheid. It is not long before the first expedition into the interior, under Johannes Steffler, sets out to find these places of reputed wealth. However, in the Lebombo mountains they are attacked and forced to return to Fort Lydsaamheid.

Another expedition, this time under Johannes Monna, is sent out. The journey takes them through the territory of Chief Matolle and where the locals run at the sight of them, already au fait with the slave-trading practices of the white man. Reaching the Matola River, they promptly rename it the Olifants River after noting the large number of these creatures on its banks. With local guides they enter Muambo, the territory of Chief Semane. Semane promises guides to take them to Chief Nassangano, who is their immediate goal.

News filters down that Nassangano has decreed that all the white intruders in the land are to be killed and any local guides who assist them severely punished. But the men carry on, lured by reports of gold and silver in an area called Coupane Ciremanelle, more gold at Beloele, and copper and ivory at Simengele. The only trouble is – Coupane lies a two-day journey away and there is no water en route. The age-old ruse continues: greed for wealth pitted against local knowledge; draw out the supply lines; weaken the enemy; and then attack! Napoleon found this out, to his cost, in Russia and it is no different here in the African interior.

The expedition passes mKamgane, Makanje, and crosses the Sonduene River (now known as the Klip), the party beset by increasingly aggressive local peoples. The Dutch try, unsuccessfully, to barter for cattle. When the locals see the beads offered they spit on the ground and leave, taking their animals with them.

The weary explorers realise that further progress is futile, although they hear, for the umpteenth time, that the mythical treasure trove is, 'merely hours away'. Their animals are weak and sick, their goods are useless for bartering and their lives at risk. It is at this point that one of the pack animals carrying most of the gunpowder falls into a river.

Then the local chief, Dawano, attacks with spears. The Dutch rally and respond with gunfire. Acting smartly, the party retires to the open plains – out of throwing, but not firing, range. With gunpowder in short supply, however, the party has to retreat even further.

Each day of the battle brings the same chilling cry from Dawano's men: *'Hotte Hotte molonge'* – 'Devour the white people!' The tribe particularly want the flintlocks which they call *Hongo Songilo* – 'magnificent sticks'. The Dutch reach the settlement of Matolle and after that, Maphumbo, where they are back on friendly territory. They march straight for Fort Lydsaamheid only to discover chaos there. Because of the terrible conditions at the fort a mutiny had been planned by a section of the men. The plot had been uncovered and 62 men were arrested. After the trial, 22 men had been executed, their bones broken with iron bars, then their heads severed from their bodies. Some had been suffocated close to death, and then beheaded. The rest had been simply hanged.

The inland chiefs – Matashaj, Mambe, Matoli, Mateke – attack. Though the fort responds as best it can, nothing can be done to stop the slaughter of the entire Dutch party, save one slave.

This failure to produce results caused the Dutch East India Company to take the remaining men out of this fated spot. Fort Lydsaamheid was abandoned and, on 27 December 1730, the men sailed for Cape Town. The fort still stands in the centre of Maputo. Between Lower Sabie and Crocodile Bridge in the Kruger you'll discover a small plaque commemorating the battle.

Lüderitzbucht

Lüderitz is a quaint town in Namibia with solid German-type residences and a mansion on the Diamantberg. They say it was built on diamonds but I say that the diamonds built it.

Today, the diamond fields lie deserted. The landscape is desolate, treeless and plagued by the dreaded south-west winds that howl down the dunes for over half the year: a place so inhospitable that all water used to be obtained from condensing seawater. Years ago, the water-distilling plant at the waterfront would process thousands of gallons of water each day, pumping it up to the reservoir on the side of Diamantberg where the mansion was built. (This building, incidentally, was erected in anticipation of a visit by the Crown Prince of Germany. The visit never materialized and it was sold to the Union Government for £1 200, to serve as a magistrate's residence.)

Never again will Lüderitz have its own stock exchange where shares worth millions change hands every day. Never again will it reverberate with the noise and bustle of lavish parties like those that the wealthy held in those diamond days, the days when a visiting schoolteacher emptied her shoes of sand, after walking on the town's outskirts, and a diamond fell out. Now, as you look out to Kolmanskop some distance away, you can almost see the abandoned machinery, costing a fortune, rusting away in the sand.

From the side of Diamantberg, looking out over the town, you see Shark Island, another place worth remembering from the time of German occupation. In 1906 the indigenous tribes of the land – the Ovambo, Bergdamara, Bondelswarts and so on – were in revolt. To the north, the Hereros had already been decimated, and it was to Shark Island that the

Germans herded the captured Hottentots. There was no hospital there for those beaten people. They arrived looking like skeletons, without blankets or clothing, and many starved to death here. Some escaped at night by sea, only to perish in the uncaring desert if they managed to reach the shore.

Present-day Lüderitz was originally 'Angra dos Ilhoes' (Bay of Islands), following Bartholomew Diaz's discovery of the site in 1486. Portuguese cartographers mistakenly referred to the colony as 'Angra Pequena', meaning 'Little Bay'. The explorer set up a traditional stone cross (at Diaz Point), where the lighthouse now stands. The original cross was shattered by drunken seamen in the early 1800s, but portions were rescued and can be seen in the South African Museum in Cape Town. In Lüderitz you can also see the skeleton of a Negro woman. This is believed to be the skeleton of a west African woman who actually sailed with Diaz. This was not unusual; it was common practice to pick local women up along the way.

In 1883, a merchant from Bremen, Adolf Lüderitz, arrived and took possession of the bay. Germany had asked the British to protect Adolf Lüderitz, as well as some German missionaries in the interior. When Britain refused, Germany annexed the desert coast, making it its first-ever colony.

And had it not been for the following story, Lüderitz would probably have remained the sleepy, dust-blown backwater it started out as:

A beachcomber, nicknamed 'Bismarck', was working guano on one of the islands when he came across a number of diamonds. He sold them in Cape Town and was immediately arrested for processing uncut diamonds. He swore blind that they were not from the Kimberley district and diamond experts verified this. But, such was the inflexible nature of the law at the time that the man spent five years in Cape Town's Breakwater Prison, probably the toughest prison in the world.

In 1908, August Stauch and a gang of rail workers were shovelling sand off the newly laid track, when one of the gang spotted something yellowish glittering in the sun. A labourer who had worked in Kimberley identified it as a diamond. Some stories say that this labourer's name was

Kolman, hence the name Kolmanskop. Stauch resigned from his company post and then pegged claims – which proved extremely profitable.

The news was out. Hungry hordes of fortune hunters rushed to this most desolate place on God's earth. Within months a roaring mining camp, complete with beer halls, hotels, shops and flaxen barmaids of dubious reputation, formed this 'New Eldorado'. Over all this floated the German Eagle.

Diamond camps arose south of Lüderitz – Elizabeth Bay, Ida Tal, Marchen Tal, Stauchlager and Pomona. However, they all followed the same fate: yielding up their millions then disappearing into the desert sands.

Old timers

I take great glee in rummaging through the old accounts of different places in South Africa, trying to reconstruct what times were like then. Take, for instance, the fact that between Boksburg and Johannesburg lay a bare and dreary farm called Elandsfontein, acquired way back in 1848 by a Mr J G Meyer in exchange for a bullock wagon. One John Jack, who owned a trading store on Lake Chrissie (today known as Chrissiesmeer), wandered across Meyer's land and tried his hand at panning. The result was that he acquired an option on the farm and he and his trading partner at Lake Chrissie, August Simmer, sank every penny they had into the venture. They employed an Australian prospector called Charles Knox and together established the renowned Simmer and Jack Goldmine.

In 1877 a town was laid on the Elandsfontein Farm to house the mineworkers. John Jack gave it the name of Germiston, in memory of the little farm near Glasgow in Scotland where he had been born.

More gold was discovered north-east of Boksburg in September 1877, on a farm then known as Benoni. A man by the name of Ethelbert Wellsford Noyce had leased this farm from the government in 1875 at a rental of £10 per year. Benoni received its name in a very odd manner. Formed from the leftover ground of two adjoining farms, its irregular shape posed many problems for the surveyor. Exasperated, the surveyor went to the Bible and borrowed Rachel's name for Benjamin – Benoni – 'the son of my sorrow' – for the farm's title. Let me assure you any sorrow the place had ever caused was soon forgotten: on 9 May 1888 it was proclaimed a goldfield and a mine called The Chimes began operating there. I think The Chimes Hotel is still in existence to this day.

Johannesburg and the surrounding area became rife with scoundrels and villains of every shape and form, carted in from all the darkest corners of the world. Speculation in claims and swindling carried on at a tremendous rate. Claim-jumping became a public menace. The law of the time stipulated that if any claim was not worked for a continuous period of 14 days it was legal to jump it – meaning one could uproot the owner's pegs and insert one's own. Furious rows ensued, for, as you can imagine, one only had to go on two weeks' leave to lose a gold mine!

A whole new profession of claim-jumping flourished on the Rand. There were scoundrels and adventurers who watched with eagle eyes for the slightest technical slip by the holder of any profitable claim. If the claim-holder paid for his licence even a minute late, or was held up in his work by the elements or for technical reasons, or exhibited even the slightest non-compliance with the letter of the law – the claim was jumped.

This racket reached its climax on 16 July 1887, when news swept Johannesburg that a large-scale attempt had been made to jump the claims held by a number of public companies, on the flimsy grounds of some supposed technical error. There was mass indignation, particularly when people learnt that the leader of the jumpers was none other than W P Fraser (of Fraser Street fame), who happened to be a leading member of the diggers' committee pledged to fight the evil of claim-jumping! A huge gathering of people took place in Marshall Square. Recognising the very real possibility that he might be lynched, Fraser hurriedly withdrew his claim. He was then taken to the claims and personally made to replace all the new pegs, accompanied by shouts of, 'Draw the pegs!' Fraser complied. The crowd moved on in search of other jumpers and an effigy of Fraser was burnt in the centre of the town before an excited throng.

A vigilante committee was subsequently formed to guard against jumping, as it was appreciated that world confidence in the Rand, which supplied it with its very necessary capital, would be shaken or totally destroyed if the troublesome practice went unchecked.

This is how the dubious profession of claim-jumping came to a sticky end in our town, but there were many other opportunities for knaves and rogues. The firing of revolvers and burglaries were both commonplace.

The famous Irish Brigade from the Eastern Transvaal moved into the Rand and started creating havoc. One of its more choice members, James Butler, was arrested on 12 February 1888 after three corpses were discovered in the centre of town – Butler being a prime suspect.

The area known as Brickfields, below the market, was the acknowledged rough section of the town, and a bar there known as The Cricketers' Arms was the unofficial 'capital' of the place. It was certainly the centre from which fights and other disturbances tended to radiate. Public houses such as The Sheba Bar, The Evening Star and The Circular Bar were just as notorious. All had elaborate systems of sentries and electric bells to warn of the approach of the police, who occasionally raided but seldom caught anyone. The only real success they had was on the night of 15 June 1899, when they raided the Tollemache Bar and luck was on their side. The electric bell wasn't working, so the police were able to tear through the bar and into the back rooms where the gambling went on.

The Central Hotel was the first stone building erected in Johannesburg, and from the day it opened it was crammed with people. As a result, a whole brood of annexes and extra rooms, equally crowded, grew up around it. The proprietors decided to add another storey to the main block and the new construction was watched with interest by the whole of Johannesburg. Bets were laid as to whether the old building could carry the new storey. It couldn't. At 1:30 a.m. on 19 January 1889 the whole place collapsed. Of three waiters sleeping on the dining-room tables, one was killed, while the other two managed to scramble out. When the ruins were examined the next day it was found that what had seemed to be walls of stone were merely shells for the inside was hollow.

Such was the façade of early Johannesburg.

Casualties of war

Walk back with me in time to witness what an average family went through in the latter stages of the Anglo-Boer War. I am indebted to Professor Ampie and his wife Bev Roos Muller for this story, as the events described concern Ampie's forefathers.

There is a farm that lies on the Bloemfontein road, just past Thaba 'Nchu, called Halt Whistle. The British came to burn it down. Back in the United Kingdom, the leader of the opposition in the House of Commons had already said, 'When is a war not a war? When we use methods of absolute Barbarity, as we are doing in South Africa!' Commandant A P J Diederichs, the owner of Halt Whistle, died in the battle of Magersfontein on 11 December 1899, and his widow, Martha, and her three daughters and two young sons saw their house burnt to the ground. As was the British custom in those days, a family had 20 minutes to salvage what they could before the troops entered and started looting and smashing.

Martha and the children did as best they could. They made an *afdak* out of corrugated iron, which they leant up against one of the still intact walls of their destroyed home. They also managed to locate several cows that were on the other side of the hill. These were herded back to the house, not the kraal, for that was full of the cattle and sheep slaughtered by the British.

One day, two of the cows did not return and Martha sent her two sons, one aged 13 and the other aged 10, to scour the countryside. By dusk, they still had not returned. The mother waited up all night but to no avail. A search for the boys the next day proved fruitless – there was neither sight nor sound of them. The mother was distraught with grief.

Albert and Roelfie (the two sons) had, during their search for the missing cattle, stumbled upon a British patrol. They were immediately captured, taken to the regiment, trained down to the coast and then shipped off to a concentration camp in Bermuda where they saw out the remainder of the war. The conditions in the camp were so bad that the younger boy, Roelfie, died of dysentery. Eventually, the war ended and Albert was shipped back to Cape Town. From the port he made his way by train to Bloemfontein. Struggling to recall the exact whereabouts of the family farm, all he could remember was that he had to walk east along the Thaba 'Nchu road.

For three days Albert walked, desperately trying to find his way home, begging food and water and sleeping by the side of the road. He knew that the farm lay somewhere between Thaba 'Nchu and Ladybrand. On the fourth day, weak with hunger, he thought he recognised a mountain – Thaba Patshoa. Ascending the beacon, he surveyed the land below, finally spotting in the distance Thaba Etelele – the place where he and his brother had looked for the cows what seemed like a lifetime ago.

Eventually, Albert falteringly approached the ruins of the once lovely homestead. An old woman there, holding an axe in her hand to deter strangers, failed to recognise the son that stood before her. It was only when Albert looked at her and said 'Mama' that it slowly dawned on the old woman that this was, indeed, her son. Her long-lost boy had come back to her.

Albert later qualified as a teacher and was posted to a school in Reitz where it is believed that his gravestone now stands.

Such is the terror and horror of war and the effects it has on the families that are torn apart by it.

How the Milky Way was formed

Once, long ago, there lived a small tribe of Bushmen in the vast plains on the edge of the Magalagadi Pans. The men would hunt while the women would look for roots and fruits to supplement their meals. When the men returned to camp, the older women would cook and the younger girls would play, often using a tsamma melon as a ball. As they played, they would sing. They would sing the song of the Grey Lourie – calling *'Kurrrr ... i Mamma ... Kurrrr ... i Mamma'* – the song of the wasp, the puffadder and the frog. But, X!Ama, a beautiful young girl, would sing her own sad song. She wore an old and ragged *karos*, full of holes where the icy winds of winter would sneak through. She felt like a shaggy Brown Hyena. She sang loudly, hoping that Gau was listening, for if Gau could kill a gemsbok or an eland she would be the happiest girl in the camp.

Gau heard her singing and watched as she tossed the tsamma back and forth with her peers. He made up his mind.

'Will you hunt with me?' he asked his friends.

'Are you mad?' came the reply. 'It is one of the hottest days of summer; where do you think that you will find animals?'

Gau filled his little water bag, collected his fire sticks and hunting gear, turned, and left.

That night he made a fire and the following morning he came across the spoor of a small herd of gemsbok. He broke into a loping jog. On and on he jogged. Another night passed. The next day, at noon, he came across them. They were standing under the scant shade of a tree in the heat of the midday Kalahari sun. The creatures knew he was there and, every now and then, one would snort and shake his head and stamp a hind foot in irratation.

Gau crept nearer and nearer, then drew his bow. He shot, knowing at once that he had hit home. The gemsbok were up and running. He did not even bother to match their pace; he just loped along, following the tracks. It was towards late afternoon when he saw the vultures circling in the hills close by. He quickened his pace for he did not want the skin to be damaged.

Gau came upon the big gemsbok male lying on the ground. He apologized to its spirit, explaining that the tribe had to survive and the spirit of the gemsbok departed. Gau made a fire then skinned the animal and cut its meat into strips, knowing how little he would be able to carry back to camp.

He set out the following morning using his spear to carry his load. But, as he travelled, he noticed that the tracks he'd followed had been swept away by the wind. Gau, being young, was not yet adept in tracking. By the end of the second day he realised he was lost. He found a waterhole, drank, and made a fire for the night.

He smelled the beast before seeing it. Then he picked up the eyes of a huge hyena, lurking just outside the perimeter of the fire.

Back at the Bushmen's camp X!Ama was now beside herself. She had initially been so excited and proud that Gau had listened to her song. Now, she found herself in the depths of remorse – it was her selfishness that had sent her beloved young man away on such a perilous mission. X!Ama could not sleep, so she sat up next to the fire, thinking, waiting, hoping, and lamenting her actions.

Gau could not reach his bow and arrows; he had left them hanging from a tree when he had gone to drink and the hyena now blocked the way. The animal lifted its head to the stars and howled, almost in victory. Smelling the human scent upon the hunting gear, the hyena reached up and plucked it from the tree. With its powerful jaws the animal snapped Gau's hunting tools in half. The young man understood he was now in desperate trouble. The hyena became more aggressive. The smell of the gemsbok meat drew it closer and closer. Gau circled the fire warily, then threw a piece of meat to the beast. Devouring the meat, the hyena then approached even nearer, halving the distance between itself and the trapped hunter.

X!Ama, sitting with her legs folded underneath her by the flames, could stand her grief no longer. Plunging her hands into the fire she grabbed the burning coals, then sprang up and threw them to the heavens, crying, 'Please, Gods of Light, help me find Gau!' As she looked at her burnt hands a strong wind came and carried the glowing coals into the sky.

The hyena was on the point of attack when Gau took a burning branch, and, in desperation, flung it at the beast. The wind took the flying sparks from the branch and joined it with the oncoming embers from X!Ama's fire. The hyena took one look at the lights that filled the sky and fled.

Gau gathered up the gemsbok skin and ran, following the path of light.

As the lights faded into the morning X!Ama saw him approaching in the distance. She fell to her knees and wept and since his return has never left his side.

And on a clear night, if you look up at the stars, you will see above you the Milky Way that Gau followed.

Modern-day Botswana

It was 21 years ago, this year, that I was offered a transfer up to Botswana to help with the setting up of a new diamond mine – to be called Jwaneng. Orapa and Letlhakane mines, in the Kgalagadi saltpans to the north, were already operating.

I remember very clearly the foresight and visionary zeal of the late Harry Oppenheimer when he stood up to make his address at the opening of the new mine. The point he made that I particularly remember was his wish that, in years to come, the people would not look at the mine and just see a huge hole in the ground. Rather, he hoped that the people would look at the hole in terms of what it had done for all concerned. By this he meant the jobs it had created, as well as the educational and infrastructural developments that it had led to. In short, everything that could be associated with the building of a winning people, nation and country. Profound words indeed.

Let's consider what Botswana was like 20 years ago. Though it had gained its independence from Britain some years previously, it was still thought of as a small, uneducated little colony living off handouts from the remnants of the old British Empire. It was rated as one of the poorest countries in the entire world, its people poverty stricken and unemployed. Boasting the most ancient people on the planet – the San, or Bushmen – it had, nevertheless, persecuted them remorselessly. The Bushmen had been hunted like wild animals and exterminated like vermin and ultimately made to settle in the inhospitable central Kalahari area, where no sane person would want to live. I have sat in a certain hotel bar in Botswana where the original license to hunt Bushmen hangs on the wall; it was issued at the beginning of the twentieth century.

Then came a humble geologist, Gavin Lamont, who unwittingly unearthed the source of Botswana's contemporary prosperity. Lamont was studying the behaviour of the Kalahari ants as they dug deep down into the earth to establish their nests, carrying the soil to the surface. What neither the ants nor Lamont knew was that the soil they transported was 'blue ground' – *diamondiferous kimberlite*. In the Naledi valley (Naledi being Venus, the evening star, and also the Goddess of Fertility), Lamont had stumbled upon what was to grow into the richest diamond mine in the world. It gives me goose bumps to relate what we glibly call 'coincidence'.

Coincidence that the richest diamond pipe on the planet is situated in the valley of the Goddess of Fertility? Coincidence that the place has the ancient Tswana name of Jwaneng, meaning 'The Place of Stones'? Coincidence that Harry Oppenheimer, the head of De Beers, links up with Sir Seretse Khama, the President of Botswana, and they both share the same vision of the future? I don't think so.

Twenty-one years later I stepped aboard a plane bound for Gabarone, the dusty, untarred capital of Botswana as I remembered it from before.

My experience was mind-blowing. Gabarone is a tarred, bustling city. The first thing that strikes you is its cleanliness; there is not a piece of litter in the street. The whole city is spotlessly clean. I walked the street that morning in absolute amazement. Everywhere I went, people greeted me courteously. They say a person's eyes are the windows to the soul. Well, I looked into the eyes of many people that morning and do you know what I saw? – peace, not anger; acceptance, not racism; politeness, courtesy and helpfulness. The economy is booming, people are being educated at an unbelievable rate and the unemployment rate remains acceptable. There are no beggars on street corners and the people carry themselves with absolute dignity. Botswana has blossomed into what I believe to be the showcase for all of Africa.

I realised that I was experiencing the very thing that the previous leaders of the Botswana Government and De Beers had so passionately begun working towards two decades before.

Jwaneng has grown into a place full of people who care. They care about themselves; they care about others; they care about their surroundings. You are left with the impression that a lot of people are doing a lot of things right in that community. From the partnership between the people of Botswana, represented by their democratically elected government, and a major industrial concern, namely De Beers, a thriving economy and society have been forged and it is awesome to behold. A government which refuses to tolerate corruption in the public or private sphere and has the interests of its people at heart can, with the support of business leaders, transform the concept of a proper and just society into a living reality.

I believe that here in South Africa we can achieve exactly what our neighbours in Botswana have: creating employment and giving our people back a sense of pride – remember that our country also possesses enormous sources of wealth. Maybe it should be compulsory for all South Africans to spend a week up in Botswana. I know what it did for me.

David Livingstone

It was on 18 April 1874 that the body of Dr David Livingstone was buried in Westminster Abbey. There had not been a funeral like it since the death of the last Prime Minister. The Prince of Wales and the current Prime Minister attended the funeral and the crowds lined Pall Mall and Whitehall.

One of his last journeys into Africa had gained international attention after *The New York Herald* had sent Henry Morton Stanley to find the ever-elusive Livingstone. Three years after that famous meeting where the immortal words 'Dr Livingstone I presume' were uttered, Livingstone was dead and his body, disguised as a bale of cloth, had been carried by his faithful followers some 2 500 km to the coast to be shipped back to Britain.

Florence Nightingale had referred to him as 'the greatest man of his generation' and to question his saintliness at that point would have been sheer madness. But, with the benefit of hindsight, let's have a look at the man.

David Livingstone was born in Blantyre, Scotland on 19 March 1813, the second of seven children in a very poor family. The beginning of the nineteenth century was a very rough time for the unlanded peasants of Scotland. The Highland Clearances had thrown the crofters off the farms of the landed gentry and into the dirt and squalor of the industrial cities to seek work. David Livingstone's grandfather had been one of these men.

A former tenant farmer on the little island of Ulva off the west coast of Mull, David's grandfather had been evicted in 1792. Moving to Glasgow, he had found work in the newly established cotton mill at Blantyre (hence the name of the town in present-day Malawi). He had been lucky;

for thousands in similar circumstances starvation or emigration were the only choices.

The company that ran the Blantyre Mill owned the tenement in which the Livingstones lived. It housed 24 families, eight on each of its three floors. Every family had a single room 14 ft by 10 ft, with two bed recesses – one for the parents and one for the children. At night, truckle beds would cover the entire floor space. Cooking, eating, reading, washing and mending all went on in this single room. There was no piped water, and slops and garbage were sloshed down crude sluice holes cut into the sides of the communal circular staircase. The rural crofters found it hard to break the habits of their farming background and, ignoring the company regulations forbidding it, kept poultry and other animals in their rooms.

David Livingstone was to remark many years later that, apart from the journey of the slaves taken into bondage, the life of the slave under an Arab master was significantly better than the lot of the poor in those teeming, dirty cities.

David started work in the cotton mill at the age of 10. Work started at six in the morning and ended at eight at night, with half an hour for breakfast and an hour for lunch. That is a working day of twelve and a half hours, six days a week – at the age of 10! Three-quarters of the work force were children and most were employed as 'piecers', their job being to 'piece' together any threads on the spinning frames that looked like breaking. It was a job that required sharp eyes and the power of constant attention. You also had to be unusually agile, since the work involved climbing under the machinery, or balancing over it. 'Piecers' walked up to 20 miles a day in the mill, mostly crawling or walking in a stooping position. Long hours spent on their feet often gave these children bowed legs and varicose veins. An adult spinner would have three 'piecers' attending his machine. As the spinner was paid according to what he produced it was in his interest to force the children on, and so spinners would often beat the children if they were not sufficiently attendant.

The steam-heated temperatures – between 80 and 90 degrees Fahrenheit – encouraged promiscuity, for to make the heat and humidity more bearable, most employees, male and female, would shed their clothes. At the end of a working day most 'piecers' were far too tired to go and play and were certainly in no frame of mind to go and learn. However, David and a handful of other children were made of sterner stuff and this is where we first pick up the metal of the young Livingstone. Defying aching limbs and tired minds, these mites would make their way to the company school and spend the next two hours learning to read and write.

Less than 10% of the child workers ever achieved any degree of literacy, and it is against this background that Livingstone's scholastic perseverance and success astounded even his schoolmaster. Already taught to read and write by his father, Livingstone started Latin during his first year of evening school. During the following few years he spent what little money he did not give to his mother on classical textbooks. In bed he would often read until midnight, his mother frequently having to take away his books. Six hours later, he would be back at the mill. There was no time for playing and David enjoyed no real childhood to speak of.

After this extremely severe upbringing, Livingstone began his first session of medical school in Anderson's College, Glasgow. This in itself was an achievement and, for somebody from his background, highly improbable. Between 1836 and 1840 he completed his medical and missionary training at the London Missionary Society.

In March 1841 Livingstone arrived in Simon's Bay in the Cape. Full of missionary zeal, he made his way up to the now celebrated Moffat's Mission Station at Kuruman, in the Northern Cape. Moffat was abroad when he arrived. Contrary to his expectations, Livingstone learnt that, over a 10-year period, Moffat had been able to convert only about 30 of the local people to Christianity. Appalled, Livingstone was convinced that the methods employed by Moffat and the other missionaries were wrong.

Livingstone made up his mind to establish his own mission station 400 km to the north, in the land of the Bagatla and the Bakwena. It is not necessary to go into what happened there. Suffice it to say that it proved a false start. During that time, Livingstone was attacked and mauled by a lion. One of his local aids, Melbewe, snatched a gun and fired both barrels, thereby saving Livingstone's life. The injured man returned to Moffat's mission to convalesce. While recuperating there, he proposed to the Moffats' daughter, Mary, who accepted.

In 1847 Livingstone set up a mission station at Kolobeng, which was under the chieftainship of Sechele. Sechele was well aware that his people were against Christianity, but he perceived in Livingstone a genuine belief in what he was trying to attain and was therefore prepared to listen to him.

Livingstone had realised that preaching to the Setswana in English was a waste of time – you might as well be talking Greek. So he set about translating some of his Christian teachings and beliefs into Setswana. This is when he encountered his first and biggest problem. Translating ethereal beliefs from one language into another is a nightmare at the best of times. For example, there is no Setswana word for 'spirit'. The closest word means 'the vapours rising from a boiling pot'. In English, we have two derivations of 'to love', one being Eros – physical or sexual love and the other being Agape – brotherly and godly love. Setswana does not have the second derivative. Thirdly, the concept of a mortal sin means the same as 'cow dung' in Setswana. And so the ironic tragedy began to unfold.

The Chief and the elders called Livingstone and asked him to demonstrate how he prayed to his God. The missionary went down on his knees in the sand, bent his back, placed his hands together and prayed. 'Ah,' the elders observed, 'now we understand – your God lives in the ground down there.'

'No,' replied Livingstone, 'He lives up there,' and pointed skywards.

'But why, when you speak to him, do you face the earth?' the elders asked, puzzled.

Livingstone went on to explain to the Chief that on resurrection day all the dead would rise, alive once more. Now that is all an African warrior chief needs to hear – that this God is going to bring back all the enemy warriors he has killed in battle!

A Livingstone sermon, for the confused Setswana, sounded something like this:

'That the God who lives in the ground will come down from the sky, accompanied by all the dead warriors that you have killed. He will then proceed to have sex with everybody because the people have cow dung on the vapours of their boiling pots.' The elders were incredulous. But with extreme politeness, as is the African way, they smiled. When alone with the Chief, however, they asked, 'How can you listen to the ravings of this madman?'

'Be quiet,' said the Chief. 'Listen to his nonsense, because he comes with guns and that is what we really need.'

Sechele converts to Christianity and is taken down along with his children to the river for baptism. The mothers are convinced that Livingstone is trying to feed the children to the crocodiles. To add insult to injury he tells the Chief that seeing that he has now converted to Christianity, the ancient rainmaking ceremonies must stop and the witch doctor be cast out of the tribe. The other chiefs and elders are outraged. The area then undergoes a two-year drought, at the end of which the elders tell the Chief that if he does not bring the rainmaker back they will rise up against him. Sechele calls the rainmaker back and, a week after the ceremony, the drought is broken and the rain cascades down. The universal sentiment is, 'So much for listening to the ranting of that white man.'

When Livingstone tells the Chief that as a Christian he is to only have one wife, pandemonium erupts. Those who understand African marriage customs and the significance of the *lobola* will appreciate the complexity of arrangements governing the use and ownership of the *lobola* cattle, and the subtleties of conduct and manner that inform the Chief's treatment of his different wives. When the Chief announces that all the wives and their offspring, barring the chief wife, are to go back to their various tribes the social fabric of the tribe is practically destroyed.

One by one the crying women, who in their own eyes have done nothing wrong, come sobbing to Livingstone. They hand him back their Bibles, saying that he must take back his book, for they want to go away and live somewhere where his God cannot come and destroy them in this cruel manner. They return in shame to the various tribes of their origin.

It is no wonder that during his life as a missionary, Livingstone managed to convert only one black man to Christianity – Chief Sechele – who, after Livingstone's departure, reverted to ancestral worship. It begins to dawn on Livingstone that, in order to maintain or increase his fame, he has to channel his energies in another direction.

In 1847 Livingstone wrote to William Cotton Oswell, a wealthy explorer, and suggested to him that they should set out to find the lake to the north-west which the locals have told him about – Lake Ngami. Oswell arrived with a companion named Mungo Murray. These two men were of similar character and neither ever bothered to press their own claims, the type who preferred to 'just do it' and let others be content to babble.

The importance of Oswell's contribution to the first trip to Lake Ngami can be gauged by the fact that when he came to Kolobeng he brought 20 horses, 80 oxen, three wagons and sufficient supplies in gunpowder, bullets, tea, coffee and sugar for a whole year. The party set out for Lake Ngami. It was thought that all previous attempts to reach the lake had failed because of the dangers posed by the Kalahari Desert. Crossed in the wrong season the Kalahari brought almost certain death. However, during the rainy season the water lies in sun-baked hollows and does not dry up until several months later. And at this time tsamma melons and red cucumbers add to the moisture source, so making it possible to cross the desert.

Livingstone was in a state of great excitement. Victorian England had no access to other European countries' records, so he had not read about Graca or Silva Porto and therefore genuinely believed that he had hit on new important information on the nature of South Central Africa. The party reached Lake Ngami but Livingstone was not satisfied: he wanted to push on to the north-east. The local chief, however, would not give permission for him to cross the Thamalakane River, nor would he supply the necessary dugouts. The reason for this was that the local chief realised that the white man would eventually meet up with Sebitoane, the chief of the war-like Makololo. This tribe had been forced westwards by the Matabele into the Barotse Valley, an area fraught with malaria and tsetse. If the white man supplied guns to Sebitoane the fragile situation would undoubtedly worsen.

Oswald offered to come back from Cape Town the next year and bring with him a collapsible boat. Livingstone agreed to this and the men turned back. In the months to come, Livingstone would claim all the accolades for the discovery of Lake Ngami. Back at Kolobeng, Livingstone could not bear the thought of anybody else penetrating further north than Ngami. So, when Oswald eventually returned to Kolobeng with the collapsible boat as promised, Livingstone had already left, taking his entire family. The children were young – Robert was four, Agnes three and Thomas one – and Mary was already five months pregnant. Despite this, Livingstone decided to cross the Kalahari at the worst possible time of the year – an insane idea!

It could not have taxed his medical knowledge to work out that Mary would probably give birth along the way. Tsetse attacked and the oxen began to sicken and die. All the children contracted fever. Livingstone later wrote that the mosquitoes were so bad that there was not half a square inch on the children's bodies left unbitten after a single night's exposure. The irony of the situation was that the chief then gave permission for them to cross the Thamalakane River but, because of sickness, they had to turn back and re-cross the Kalahari.

On one occasion they all went without water for two whole days; the children's lips cracked and burst and their tongues, swollen in their mouths, turned black. By the time they reached Kolobeng no one could stand unassisted. Mary was in a terrible state. Try to imagine going through the last months of your pregnancy in a jolting wagon, eating a totally unbalanced diet, having little and sometimes no water to drink, suffering the searing heat of the Kalahari and seeing your children too ill to stand.

Back at Kolobeng, the new baby daughter arrived. She contracted a bronchial infection and died, screaming in pain. The family went to the Moffats in Kuruman to convalesce. Mary Moffat, Mary Livingstone's mother, discovered, in April 1851, that her daughter was pregnant again. Upon hearing that Livingstone planned yet another trip to Ngami with his family, she wrote him a letter (which survives to this day), openly telling him how self-centred and uncaring he is of his wife and family. This made Livingstone more determined than ever to go ahead.

Livingstone now had a new dream – he imagined a navigable highway, starting from Luanda in Angola and stretching past the Victoria Falls, all the way down to the east coast of Mozambique at the mouth of the Zambezi.

Arriving at the little town of Linyanti on the Chobe River, Livingstone noticed that some of the clothing worn was made of European cloth – one or two locals even proudly sported dressing gowns.

He was told that these were traded from a north-western tribe known as the Mambari in the area around Bie in Central Angola, 1 000 km north-west of Linyanti. Livingstone learnt that these Mambari were acting as middlemen and agents for the Portuguese – practised slave traders – in Angola.

The British Empire had abolished slavery in 1833. But, barely twenty years later, when Livingstone reached the heart of South Central Africa, there were still some 60 000 slaves crossing annually from West Africa to Brazil, Cuba and the southern states of America. Although nations such as Portugal, Spain and France had officially outlawed slavery, in practice they turned a blind eye to its continuation. Livingstone was forced to acknowledge that even the Makololo were not averse to participation in it.

Livingstone's position had now become painfully ironic. He had come hoping to find an untouched people. Instead, he was confronted by the reality that they had already been tainted by external influences and that he, advocating further contact with outsiders, would undoubtedly contribute to their corruption.

In April 1852 Livingstone journeyed down to Cape Town and put Mary and the children on a ship bound for England. He had written to the directors of the London Missionary Society asking them to keep his family. Although he said that parting from his children was like tearing out his entrails, it was Mary and the children who suffered four years of absolute poverty and helplessness, a situation which eventually drove his wife to drink – a habit that she did not break until her death some ten years later. Mary was obliged to beg for money and to move her long-suffering children all over the country in search of housing. In letters to her husband she pleaded for him to come home.

Livingstone returned to Linyanti and found that the Makololo had a new chief called Sekeletu. With Sekeletu's assistance Livingstone began a journey of almost 2 000 km up the Zambezi Valley, then headed west for Angola and the Port of Luanda. As he travelled Livingstone encountered many tribes, each with their own specific customs, rites and social structures – the Balobale (an aggressive tribe led by a woman), the Mambari and the Balonda, for example.

Every step of the way Livingstone had to pay for passage and his supplies of beads, wire and ivory were consumed rapidly. He was perpetually sick with fever and at one point wrote, 'Everything moves to the left and if I don't hold onto something, I fall to the ground.' Quinine supplies were low.

Livingstone had heard that there were a number of Englishmen in Luanda. Close to death, he was carried into Luanda on 1 May 1854 and found a single Englishman – a Mr Edmund Gabriel, who sported the impressive title of 'Her Majesty's Commissioner for the Suppression of the Slave Trade in Luanda'. Unable to write a full-length letter, Livingstone dictated one to Edmund Gabriel, in which he reassured the London Missionary Society that he was, indeed, still alive. He related how he had battled through forests, swamps, hostile tribes, slavers and constant fever yet told the directors that it was his intention to turn back to Linyanti and, from there, undertake a similar trip, this time on the east coast.

Livingstone was back in England from December 1856 to March 1858. The adulation received was astonishing, even excessive. The Royal Geographic Society presented him with its Gold Medal, an Honorary Degree from Oxford followed, and, to top it all, he enjoyed a private audience with Queen Victoria. His book, *Missionary Travels and Researches in South Africa*, published in November 1857, sold 70 000 copies, making him both rich and famous. A series of public lectures throughout the country followed. With all this activity, his wife and children saw very little of him during that time. They had spent four and a half years in squalor prior to his return.

The London Missionary Society decided to open another mission station at Linyanti. It was to be headed up by Holloway Helmore, who was the resident missionary at Letakoo, north-east of Kuruman. Helmore and nine other Europeans made the journey. They arrived at Linyanti at the worst time for fever – February. Seven of the nine perished within the first two months.

Sekeletu's handling of the new missionaries was nothing short of appalling – he refused to let them cross the Chobe until they had handed over all their clothes and possessions. The guides that he supplied led the spans of oxen into tsetse country and they all died. But the worst treatment of all was meted out to a Mrs Price, the wife of another missionary. It was recorded that prior to her death she was so ill and thin that she used to put plasters on her joints to stop the bones from breaking through her skin. When she and her children died from fever, Sekeletu had her head severed from the corpse and presented to him. Roger Price, her husband, and two of their seven children were the sole survivors of this expedition.

Sekeletu harboured bitter feelings against Livingstone, for Livingstone had promised his men back within the year and he had now waited four. When Livingstone did eventually lead the expedition back to Linyanti he discovered, for the first time, the Kebrabasa Rapids. Their enormous height convinced him that he'd been a fool to imagine that the Zambezi could be navigable from the east coast, right up to the Batoka Plateau. There would never be the hordes of traders that he had promised Sekeletu.

In the mean time, Livingstone had resigned from the London Missionary Society and accepted the post of a roving British Consul in Mozambique on a salary of £500 per annum.

The Government sent him a little steamer which he called the *Ma-Roberts* – the name that the Makololo tribe had given his wife. In March 1858, the *Ma-Roberts*, with Mary and her youngest son Oswald on board, together with the steamship *Pearl*, headed for Mozambique. The rest of the children were left with their grandparents. On board the steamer was Captain Benningfield, who would take charge of the *Ma-Roberts*, Dr John Kirk and Richard Thornton, a geologist. The party's aim was to set out and explore the shire highlands on the way to Lake Nyasa, although they would in time encounter another set of rapids – the Murchison Rapids – that would block their passage.

On reaching Lake Nyasa, Livingstone met the warring Ajawa and Manganja tribes. They also practised slave trading, acting as middlemen for the Portuguese. Mary became severely ill and her alcoholism continued unabated.

Passing slave gangs on their trek, the party bore witness to a number of grotesque sights. At one point they came across a woman hanging from a tree. Because she was unable to keep up with the other slaves, her master had hanged her – not wanting his slave to become the property of another. Other groups of corpses were regularly found, some stabbed to death, others left tied together to die of starvation. Local people would follow the caravans, rescue those still living, feed them up and sell them back into slavery.

Mary's condition worsened, and, no longer responding to the quinine, she passed away.

Then there was the infamous meeting with Henry Morton Stanley from *The New York Herald*. Stanley stayed with Livingstone for five months and returned a hero. Livingstone, as we know, pressed on to discover the source of the Nile. He had become extremely ill. Two of his men, Susi and Chuma, constructed a litter and carried him to a little village on the banks of the river Molilamo, where he made the last entry in his journal. Livingstone was discovered the next morning on his knees by the side of his bed. The humble men waited respectfully. Eventually they approached and touched him. He was dead and had been for a couple of hours.

They buried his entrails and salted his body. Then, over a five-month period, Livingstone's corpse was carried to the Portuguese coast, from where the body was shipped back to England. The 60 loyal men, their mission accomplished and paid for, slipped quietly back from whence they had come. It was a whole year before Susi and Chuma were taken to London to visit the grave of their departed hero.

Isn't it strange in life that the real heroes, the ones who do the real work, are never rewarded? Very few of those 60 loyal men who followed him ever received the medals struck for them by the Royal Geographic Society – they simply couldn't be found.

Death of a chief

There are many stories about the old Transvaal (which was then known as the Zuid-Afrikaansche Republiek) that are erroneous and need to be clarified. One of the most misguided says that the entire Transvaal area was totally devoid of people when the voortrekkers arrived. Nothing could be further from the truth; historical, archaeological and social evidence disproves this completely.

What we do have, in fact, is a history of local peoples being systematically displaced and areas taken over, at the barrel of the gun. One such displacement took place in the area surrounding Tzaneen, Haenertsberg and Duiwelskloof in the north of our country …

Chief Magoeba was liberally referred to as a 'troublesome chief'. What that meant, in real terms, was that he refused to kow-tow, give up his land or allow his people to become itinerant labourers for the white farmers who were busy taking over. There had been an earlier campaign in the Blouberg district, where Chief Malaboch had been starved out and the Bahananoa tribe completely subjugated. That was in May 1894; Magoeba's troubles date from June 1895.

The Commandant General of the Transvaal militia was Piet Joubert and it was his task to bring this recalcitrant chief to heel. He had with him, as part of his force, Swazi and Shangaan mercenaries. Joubert ordered the Bantu under his command to tie a white band around their foreheads as a distinguishing mark. It was not long before Magoeba's spies had picked this up. The command swiftly went out for all the chief's warriors to get a piece of white cloth and tie it to their foreheads. Within a matter of hours, with everyone now wearing this decoration and no one being able to distinguish friend from foe, mayhem erupted.

The original plan of attack, as per usual, involved the black mercenaries penetrating the thick bush, like beaters at a pheasant shoot, to flush out the enemy. The commandos, patrolling the forest paths, would then intercept Magoeba and his men as they fled before the advancing line of mercenaries. Maybe it is better to let one Bernhard Dicke continue the story, which he left us in his diary:

'A party of Magoeba's men had put white bands around their foreheads. When this was brought to the attention of the Commander, they did not believe the message at all, but when the first bullet went through Commandant Barent Vorster's hat, and the second one grazed the tree where Captain Schiel was standing, they realised their predicament, and then indiscriminate firing started from all sides and pandemonium broke out.'

An avalanche of fleeing humanity, consisting of over 400 whites and 3 500 black mercenary soldiers, had now lost their heads and were running down the mountainside – a fact that went unreported in the press. The score: 15-0 to Magoeba.

On that following Sunday – 9 June – while most of the Boers were at church, a large party of Swazis went hunting Chief Magoeba. They ran into two young wives of Magoeba and tortured them. One eventually broke down and told them that Magoeba was hiding in a densely wooded kloof half way up the Wolkberg. The Swazis went there as fast as they could. Magoeba was waiting for them. One of the party received a full blast of a double-barrelled rifle and fell dead beside his comrades. The second barrel misfired and, while the chief was struggling to reload, a Swazi mercenary of unknown name took aim and brought him down.

As Magoeba lay dead at their feet the men argued about how they were going to convince the white men that he had actually been killed. Their answer was to cut off Magoeba's head and carry it in a woven basket up the mountainside to General Joubert's camp. There was a professional photographer there, named Exton, who took a photograph of Magoeba's severed head. The photograph exists to this day. (At a later date, an artist named Astley Maberly painted the head from studying the photograph.)

President Kruger was purportedly very upset by the fact that Chief

Magoeba's head had been cut off on a Sunday and he gave Joubert a severe reprimand. The total number of casualties on the campaign to destroy Magoeba and his people was 13 killed and 18 wounded – all black mercenaries. There was not a single white casualty.

Kruger told the Volksraad that it should set aside R20 000 to be distributed amongst the mercenaries who had participated in the fight. The Volksraad was horrified by this request. In the end, the leaders of the black forces received R4 each and their soldiers R2. The 4 000 followers of Magoeba, Mamathola, Moshouti and Tslobolo were put to work on the now white-owned farms in the area. With the death of Magoeba, severe punishment was meted out to the 'rebellious tribes'. In most cases a fine of R10 was levied against every adult male, which, of course, paid for the costs of the campaign. The descendants of those subjugated tribes still live in the area surrounding Magoeba's Kloof.

Now, maybe we can begin to understand why there is such an outcry for land reform in various parts of our country. It is an issue that must be addressed and rectified if we are to build a new and prosperous nation together.

Big-hearted men and little boats

I doubt if there is anyone alive who can still recall Captain J C Voss, a Canadian, who sailed a dugout canoe from British Columbia all the way across the oceans to England on a voyage that included a brief, though entertaining, stay in our country.

It was on a summer's morning in 1904 that the keeper of the lighthouse at Cape Point was surprised to see a threemasted, schooner-rigged canoe sailing past! This highly original craft had been hollowed out of a massive red cedar tree trunk by Alaskan Indians and was some 10 m in length. She drew only 40 cm of water. The bowsprit incorporated the carved figure of an American Indian. The narrow hull could carry 450 l of water and sufficient provisions for three months.

Voss had bought the canoe for a few pounds and a jar of whisky off an Alaskan Indian. He acquired it to prove that, if fitted out correctly, a small craft could ride out any weather. To facilitate this Voss had added a lead keel, some ballast, a deck and a total of three masts – capable of carrying 21 square metres of sail. The only trouble was that if anyone climbed the mast the canoe heeled over! Voss had also designed a very special sea anchor for the voyage – this was to stand him in good stead. The canoe held the grand title of *Tilikum*.

When he started the initial journey, from British Columbia to Australia, Voss's first shipmate fell overboard into the Pacific, taking with him the only compass. Incredibly, Voss completed his passage to Sydney using only the sun and the stars as navigational aids.

When he reached Durban, just after Christmas 1903, a tug master hailed him as he sailed into the harbour.

'Where are you from?' shouted the tug master.

'Victoria, British Columbia,' Voss replied.

'Good God man, you have nerve!' the tug master exclaimed.

'Necessary, if you want to get along in the world!' came the response.

A friend of Voss's suggested that he should take the *Tilikum* up to the Transvaal, so he had it railed up and it was put on display at the Wanderers Cricket Ground as 'the first deep-sea vessel ever to visit Johannesburg'.

Strangely enough, it was when it was travelling on dry land that an accident befell the *Tilikum*: while the boat was being transported to Pretoria one of the horses took fright at the Indian figurehead and promptly kicked it off! General Louis Botha, visiting the exhibition in Pretoria, shook Voss's hand before remarking, 'I would rather go through another Boer War than cross the ocean in the *Tilikum*!'

Voss then transported the *Tilikum* by rail to East London where he set sail for Algoa Bay. On arrival, a fleet of full-rigged sailing ships on the beaches greeted him. A gale drove him into Mossel Bay and another was encountered at Danger Point (very close to where HMS *Birkenhead* went to Davy Jones's locker), but the well-designed sea anchor did its job. There were more close encounters on the way – a whale breached and towered over him, almost swamping the tiny vessel; the boat was stabbed by sword fish; and sharks were ubiquitous companions for hundreds of kilometres. But it was when Voss fell ill with stomach cramp that he almost fell overboard. Without medication, he took mustard and warm water which, he claimed, cured him!

And so it was that the *Tilikum*, with a gentle southerly wind in her sails, came past Cape Point lighthouse and on into Table Bay. Thousands paid to see her in the circus tent in Cape Town. Voss found a new shipmate, Harrison, and the two mariners sailed away laden with presents from well-wishers: roast chickens, turkeys and geese, wines, brandies and whiskeys. Just off Robben Island they anchored for a feast.

Captain Voss had intended to set course for Pemnambuco (a port on the Brazilian coast), but Harrison became so seasick that Voss had to sail to St Helena instead, where he deposited his ailing companion. The *Tilikum* made Pemnambuco safely, after which, believe it or not, she crossed the Atlantic again, heading for England. She sailed up the English Channel and eventually ended her voyage at Margate on the Kent coast. The *Tilikum* had sailed over 64 000 km in just under three years.

As for Captain Voss, he died in 1922 at the age of 64 – a poor bus-driver. It somehow seems unfair that after such an extraordinary feat of seamanship both fame and fortune should elude this brave man.

Birth of a mining town

If you take the N12 highway out of Johannesburg, after passing the towns of Potchefstroom and Stilfontein you will find yourself on the top of a hill looking down over the town of Klerksdorp. I stopped there not so long ago and contemplated its history.

Klerksdorp came into being with the arrival of the first voortrekkers in the Transvaal, in about 1838. One Mr C M du Plooy settled on the banks of the Schoonspruit (so called because of its clear waters) and after affirming his position by force over the local tribes, set himself up on a 16 000 hectare farm, called Elandsheuvel. There is a suburb in the town by the same name today. In time, other trekkers filtered into the area, hungry for land and wealth and prepared to fight for it. It disturbs me to note that so many places in our country were, like Klerksdorp, founded upon the guiding principles of force and greed – gunpowder and gold.

These new trekkers received the rights for half of Du Plooy's farm in exchange for building a dam and water furrows for irrigation. There they settled in wattle-and-daub houses and named the town Klerksdorp, after one Barend le Clerq who was the patriarch of the early settlement.

It remained a quiet rural village, very much in the pattern of all early settlement towns. For, in spite of their sins, the first thing that the voortrekkers did when establishing any town was to build a church and a school. There was also a good-sized store, run by James Taylor and Thomas Leask, which became very well known as it supplied virtually every commercial commodity to the surrounding population.

Then came the velvet-coated vice. In 1885 traces of gold were found on Ysterspruit farm by one Van Vuuren and then, in August 1886, A P Roos found gold on the town commonage. The boom was underway. Locals named the field the Schoonspruit Goldfields and it was soon regarded as the new Barberton of the Transvaal. In July 1888, over 4 000 new diggers from across the globe drew lots for the rights to mine the townlands. With corrugated iron loaded on the backs of their wagons, they erected what today would look like an informal settlement. This caused the town to sprawl out in all directions, with no thought given to town planning, green areas or the establishment of an orderly, permanent village.

Close your eyes and picture the scene: the rush of ox wagons arriving with all sorts of impedimenta and settling in a virtually treeless dust bowl and everybody clean mad for the muck called gold; the music halls; the dance girls who hire themselves out for the biggest pile of gold dust; the square-faced bottles of gin; the Cape Smoke brandy; and the drunken revelry that inevitably surfaced in communities of this nature.

At the beginning of 1889 there were over 200 commercial buildings, 69 canteens and, believe it or not, Klerksdorp's own Stock Exchange (which today is the local museum). But the gold in the area was of low grade and this, coupled with the discovery of the Witwatersrand, began the exodus. Most of the companies floated to exploit the Klerksdorp reefs were over-capitalised. Unable to show profits on such inferior-quality ore, many went bankrupt. By the end of 1889 the boom was over.

It was, in fact, maize production by the local farming community that slowly began to revitalize the region commercially. The old Central Western Cooperative Company used to be the largest of its kind in the southern hemisphere and the second largest in the world. As you survey the landscape surrounding this little town, the silos and elevators speak of an area still dominant in the business of grain production. Klerksdorp had a lifeline thrown to it when the gold ran out, as opposed to some of the little mining towns that simply crumbled into nothingness after the rush.

Incidentally, the small town just outside Klerksdorp called Stilfontein had a very interesting beginning. When gold was discovered there by the Anglo Vaal company, it approached the municipality of Klerksdorp and asked for special rates and taxes. As a *quid pro quo* it was going to house all its people for the new Hartebeestfontein Mine in the town of Klerksdorp. The town council, demonstrating an acute lack of vision, refused the reduced rates and so the newcomers built their own town, which they called Stilfontein. The mines stopped producing many years ago. However, the beautiful little town, in an act of commercial genius, converted itself into an old-age retirement destination, where a three-bedroom house with garage can be purchased for around R30 000. What a great idea!

Siener van Rensburg

Nothing could be stranger than the story of the Afrikaner Nostradamus known as Siener van Rensburg. Nicolaas van Rensburg, called 'Klaasie' as a child, was born on 30 August 1864 and grew up on Rietkuil Farm, outside Ottosdaal in North West Province. He went to school at the age of seven. His father, however, needed Klaasie on the farm and brought him home after three weeks. He never went to school again. But, with the help of his mother, he learnt to read the Bible, one word at a time.

Klaasie was a fragile child and very timid. His father, Willem, was a hard and difficult man known as 'Kort Koos' because of his temper. He rejected his son, considering him a sissy. Every morning, Klaasie took his Bible and some food and went into the veld to tend the sheep, this being the only job his father deemed him fit for. As a result of his father's indifference towards him, Klaasie and his mother developed a very close bond, though he remained a terribly lonely little boy.

Klaasie had his first vision at the age of seven. While his father was away, one of the farmworkers came to warn Annie, Klaasie's mother, that a Korana gang leader named Skeelkoos was planning to attack their homestead that night. Annie started to make arrangements to flee. However, the young boy told his mother that God had come to him in a dream, saying that He would protect them but only if they remained in the house that night. Klaasie refused to be persuaded to leave so his mother decided to stay, along with Klaasie and her other three children. Klaasie stayed awake all night. At first light, the family saw Skeelkoos and his henchmen approach the house. Then, for some unknown reason, the would-be intruders suddenly turned tail and fled and the house and family went unscathed.

During the Boer War Nicolaas served under Koos de la Rey and while on commando near Kimberley at the beginning of the conflict, he had a terrible vision. Late one morning Siener was found under a bush in a terrible state, his hair and beard dishevelled, his fingernails torn and bleeding from scrabbling in the earth and his eyes red from crying. Saying that he'd nearly gone mad through battling with Satan during the night, Nicolaas went on to describe the vision he'd experienced.

He'd seen Boers fleeing over blackened earth. All the Boer women and children were in one large crowd – the children crying bitterly and the women desperate – as the British soldiers harried them. The people were surrounded by burning farmsteads and fields and the whole country lay ablaze before his eyes. Van Rensburg's apocalyptic prophecy became a reality two years later when the British implemented their 'scorched-earth' policy across the country. Burning over 2 000 farmsteads in the Free State alone and incarcerating women and children in concentration camps which would ultimately claim 27 000 lives, Britain's treatment of the Boers was every bit as nightmarish as Siener van Rensburg had pictured it to be.

His visions of the Boers being defeated, in the instance just described and on other occasions, did not go down well with everyone. One significant figure who did believe and respect him, however, was General Koos de la Rey. But, as opinion on Van Rensburg continued to be divided, the Hervormde Kerk in Lichtenburg eventually decided to find out whether Siener was a man of God or a false prophet. They appointed General de la Rey and one Dominee du Toit to conduct an investigation. On route to Siener's farm, one of De la Rey's horses, Bokkie, developed a problem so Koos borrowed another to pull his cart. When the men arrived at Siener's farm, Nicolaas asked where his old friend Bokkie was. When De la Rey asked why, Siener replied that he had been confronted by an image of De la Rey leaving Lichtenburg with Bokkie. De la Rey was astounded and he never questioned the man's ability again.

Siener was active in the failed rebellion of 1914. Many of the leaders, including Siener, were caught and jailed in the old fort in Johannesburg. Several witnesses testified that it was Siener's visions that had fuelled the rebellion. At his trial the magistrate chastised him, also offering his opinion that it was an excess of red meat in his diet that prompted the visions. Siener replied that he could not help it and that he was having one right now.

'What do you see?' the magistrate asked.

'I see that my son has died,' Siener replied.

He added that he also saw his wife in black clothes and a funeral cortège passing. It was then that a court orderly walked in and handed a note to the judge. After reading the message, the judge regarded Siener with no little pity and said, 'I regret to tell you that your son has died.'

Of course the most noteworthy of his predictions concerned the death of De la Rey, which he described to the general. He related that he'd seen a white piece of paper with the numbers one and five hanging over Lichtenburg. He'd also pictured a train carrying De la Rey's wife, Nonnie, making frequent stops where it would be surrounded by grief-stricken people. Finally, he described witnessing a man of great importance returning to South Africa, placing his sword on the ground and refusing to pick it up again.

General Beyers – the man of great importance – had been abroad and on his return to the country had resigned as Commandant General of the Union Defence Force. And as we all know, it was on the 15 September 1914 that the beloved Koos de la Rey was fatally shot, passing through a police cordon at Langlaagte in Johannesburg. All the trains, draped in black, converged on Lichtenburg for the funeral.

Potter's Hill

On a district road between Memel in the Free State and Charlestown in KwaZulu-Natal there is a lone monument on the slopes of Majuba Mountain. Translated from Afrikaans it reads, 'Erected in memory of Fanny Knight and G Roets who were shot by S Swart on May 6 1927, while he had escaped from the Police at Potters Hill.' The story attached to the monument is compelling, though gruesome.

In 1920 Stefanus Swart arrived in the area with a herd of stallions for sale. Having a previous conviction for stock theft meant Swart didn't attract too many purchasers. However, he did manage to sell a horse to a widow named Annie Eksteen, the owner of Potter's Hill Farm. Knowing which side his bread was buttered on, Swart married her, despite the mid-thirties groom being 30 years younger than his bride.

Swart was an angry man, subject to frequent violent outbursts and unprovoked quarrels. Stefanus became cross with Willie Knight, his stepson-in-law, when Annie rented a nearby farm to him for only one pound per month. A giant of a man, Swart thrashed Knight to the point where Willie had to draw a revolver to protect himself. Swart received 18 months in prison for assault. In jail, Swart developed his persecution complex – everything and everyone was against him – and a belief that he stood above the law.

Though abusive and hostile to people, Swart loved his animals. Once, catching a farm worker kicking one of his dogs, Swart reached for his gun – the farmhand had to hotfoot it over the horizon.

Swart regarded himself as something of a ladies' man and, though most women feared him, there were those attracted to a man of his nature. Swart used to flaunt his affairs in front of his elderly wife. On one occasion he locked his wife and nephew, Alwyn Visser, who was also the farm manager, in a dark room and threatened their lives. This was because Swart was having a relationship with a 17-year-old relative whom he had brought to live in the house, and charges of incest were imminent. Visser escaped with his life only after promising not to give evidence against him and Mrs Swart took flight to Potchefstroom. When the charge of incest was duly pressed, Swart ignored the summons. The die was cast.

On Tuesday 3 May 1927, Swart went to sort Knight out once and for all. But Knight had fled, forewarned. Incensed, Swart returned home and shot his beloved dogs.

The district Commandant of Volksrust was Captain Gerald Ashman. Joined by the Head Constable of Newcastle, William Mitchell, together with 12 policemen – including officers Feucht, Grove and Van Wyk – and Alwyn Visser, Ashman assembled his forces at the Belgravia Hotel in Charlestown. After discussing the matter, the men decided to split into two groups, one to work up the hillside, the other to comb the hill from the top down.

They began their hunt as the mists descended on Potter's Hill and they moved like ghosts through the murky conditions. Constable Feucht spotted Swart, only to lose sight of him again. Then, 20 yds away in a mealie field, a shot rang out and Feucht fell. Crossman and Mitchell crept up to the corner of the kraal wall, thinking Swart was hiding there. He wasn't; he was in the field behind them. The first shot wounded Crossman and Mitchell, as he dashed for cover, was brought down. Swart walked up to the stricken men and dispatched them in cold blood.

Sergeant Grove was an expert tracker and the finest shot of the party. He began tracking Swart through the mealie fields, but in the mist the hunter became the hunted and Grove was shot from behind. Swart next shot Van Wyk where he stood in the road. Ashman returned fire but Swart gunned him down as well. Swart then strolled up to Van Wyk and put a bullet in his head and another in his heart. Next, finding a horse tethered to a fence, Swart mounted and road towards Charlestown.

The news of the bloodbath had reached Charlestown and the inhabitants were panicking. Fanny Knight was worried about her husband and her children and she persuaded Roets to drive her to them in a trap. A black man who lived in a hut 50 yds from the road, on the southern slope of Majuba, watched as Mrs Knight's trap came over the ridge, while, from the other direction, he saw Swart galloping up very fast. Swart forced the trap to stop and shot Fanny Knight and Roets. The monument that I spoke of at the beginning of this story is erected on the spot where they were slain.

Swart then arrived at the farm of a Lucas van Vuuren, where he suspected his wife to be staying. He stormed through the house shouting for her. There followed two shots: one through Annie's chest and the other through her forehead. By now, however, additional police from Mount Prospect and Newcastle had arrived and they began to close in on Swart. As the police neared Badenhorst, Swart was seen. An officer named Kriel took Swart down as he began to run and he pitched into a sloot. They found Swart lying on top of his rifle with Ashman's Webley revolver in one hand. The inquest revealed that he had shot himself with his own pistol.

They buried Fanny Knight and Annie Swart at the small cemetery at Potter's Hill. At a separate funeral, the five policemen were buried with military honours. Over 2 000 mourners attended. The body of Captain Ashman was placed on an old gun carriage drawn by a police horse. Ashman's horse followed the gun carriage with the dead man's boots reversed and strapped into the stirrups.

A chilling coda to the story concerns the celebration of an African wedding in the Majuba area, when the bridal party used the Swart/Roets monument as a focal point for the wedding photographs. A picture was taken of the bridegroom leaning against the plinth yet, on developing the film, the plinth had disappeared from the picture. In its place stood the forlorn figure of a white woman dressed in old-fashioned clothing – the ghost of Fanny Knight.

The *Grosvenor* and her castaways

For centuries South Africans have been fascinated by the tale of the *Grosvenor*, her fate, and the fabulous treasure she was said to hold. It is only in very recent times that many more facts and accounts have been discovered, which allowed a South African author, now living and working in England, to piece together the full account of the *Grosvenor*. Stephen Taylor tells the story magnificently in his latest book, *The Caliban Shore*. Here's what transpired.

The *Grosvenor* was a smaller version of those great old warships called 'the 64-gun ships of the line'. She was pierced for 26 cannon and could look after herself if need be. Her apple-cheeked hull was designed to carry cargo (she could carry up to 750 000 lbs of tea) anywhere in the world. Furthermore, she was an owner's dream as her accommodation was the closest thing to luxury travel at that time.

When finished, the *Grosvenor* had used the timber of 740 mature oak trees, all over a hundred years old and grown in the old clay soils of Sussex. For every completed ton of those early vessels a single oak was required. No wonder that oak had become such a strategic resource and a bone of contention between trading companies and the Navy. She was designed for a crew of 105, all trained for naval combat.

The captain and his officers, depending upon rank, would try to accumulate wealth by over-charging the passengers for accommodation. On this particular return voyage the captain of the *Grosvenor* had done very well. He had a total of 35 passengers aboard, and none had paid more handsomely than William Hosea, travelling with his new wife, Mary. Hosea was on the verge of being caught for fraudulent trading in India. Desiring an extra swift exit, he was prepared to pay a very large sum.

The *Grosvenor* sailed from Calcutta to Madras and then on to Trincomalee. The administrator of the East, Lord Macartney, had been offended by the captain's attitude and delayed the vessel's departure for some months. They eventually sailed, under the initial escort of Admiral Hughes, on 14 June 1782 with 140 souls on board. The *Grosvenor* was at sea for 52 days after leaving Trincomalee.

At this point something needs to be said about navigation techniques of the period. The British trading maps were based upon the Portuguese Roteira charts, which were drawn up almost two centuries before. These charts were terribly flawed and showed the treacherous south-eastern African coast quite a few degrees west of where it actually lay. Furthermore, the chronometer – a vital piece of navigational equipment – was not yet available. The combination of these factors was to prove disastrous for those on board the *Grosvenor*.

To compensate for this lack of knowledge captains would leave Trincomalee on the Ceylon coast and head almost due south, right down to 40 degrees south. Then they would bear right and sail due west until 0 degrees, so ensuring that they had actually rounded the Cape. This time, however, Captain John Coxon of the *Grosvenor* miscalculated and, somewhere around 30 degrees south, turned west. The ship had turned westwards far too soon and unbeknown to Coxon, his crew and the passengers – who were all battling the storms and gale-force winds – her fate had been sealed. Her main mast had been badly sprung during the storm and the vessel was under very reduced sail – remember that a ship takes twice as long to respond to the helm when under reduced canvas.

Suddenly, a black mass of land was spotted. The captain ordered the ship to be brought about and the boatswain piped for all hands on deck. The sailors were urged to hoist more sail in the hope of improving the ship's manoeuvrability. The frantic attempts to avoid disaster lasted only a few minutes: the *Grosvenor* struck just after 4:30 a.m. on 4 August 1782.

There was an ancient ritual amongst the sailors of those times. When you were wrecked, you would make your way down into the holds of the ship, knock out the bungs of the rum kegs and drink yourself into oblivion, rather than face death by a shark feeding frenzy. But this did not happen on the *Grosvenor*: it was the look in the eyes of the women and children that seemed to stop the seamen. Then they saw it – a dark black mass – land! The penny dropped: they were not stuck out on some distant reef far from the coast but had hit land. There was still hope, a chance of life.

The *Grosvenor* had, on her return journey from India, run aground on the Pondoland coast at what is now the Mkambati Reserve on the east coast of South Africa. Within 15 minutes the water was up to the gun deck. Two light craft were called for and the jolly boat, which was about 3 m in length, was brought on deck. But the waves were breaking over the side and the jolly boat was swept up the quarterdeck and smashed to pieces against the roundhouse door. That left the yawl, a smaller craft that could carry only 12 people at a time. Lowered over the side, she too was immediately dashed to pieces.

Robert Ray, the bo'sun, ordered the men to start making a raft. Coxon, along with the more wealthy of the passengers, offered great rewards to anybody who would swim to the shore with the end of a line. Two Italians, Pandolpho and Barchini, came forward and were lowered into the water with lines clenched between their teeth. The entire ship watched, spellbound, as the two bodies headed out into the surf, their heads bobbing up and down. Barchini was almost at the rocks when a huge wave picked him up and dashed him against the black mass with a sickening force – the first of those on the Grosvenor to die. Pandolpho, however, just managed to make it to the beach. A cheer arose from the ship – they now had a line to land! Next, three Lascars plunged in, also carrying lines, and made their way along the first line. Now, with four lines on shore, the men were able to drag a hawser onto the land. Things were starting to look up when, suddenly, all discipline on board collapsed. A dozen men swarmed onto the hawser, causing it to sag in the middle, and with the waves breaking over it they were washed to their death.

William Hosea, mentioned earlier as one of the more affluent passengers, had the presence of mind to go to the captain's safekeeping box and retrieve the diamonds that he was taking home. These were valued at upwards of £10 000 in those days: a small fortune.

By midday the *Grosvenor* was in her death throes. Her stern was still impaled and her head bent deep in the water. She was gently sliding onto her beams ends when her great oak timbers started to crack up and, with a thunderous clap, she broke in the middle. There were still about 120 people on board.

The gale had blown itself out by mid-afternoon. All those still on board were huddled on the starboard quarter which suddenly lifted, miraculously cleared the reef and floated free. The quarter, seething with bedraggled women and children, rich passengers together with common seamen, started slowly drifting towards the shore. Excitement grew as the men pulling on the hawser realised that they could guide the floating portion into a little sheltered inlet. As it came towards the beach, the men jumped into the shallows and helped the women and children off the floating piece of wreckage. Once on shore, the survivors fell to their knees, numbed by the experience of setting foot again on solid earth after such a harrowing ordeal.

The casualties were mainly those who had struck out from the ship trying in vain to save themselves, and these included 14 members of the crew. Of the 105 crew, 91 had landed alive and of the 35 passengers that had set sail two months before from Trincomalee in India, only one small boy had drowned.

In the gathering gloom of their first evening ever in Africa, the group spotted a number of half-naked local tribesmen silhouetted against the skyline. The two groups watched each other with mutual incomprehension: the one party dishevelled castaways from a faraway land, and the other black warriors with high conical hairstyles, their faces smeared with red ochre mud. This was at Lambasi Bay, in the southern portion of the Mkambati Reserve.

Among the many paintings inspired by the tale of the *Grosvenor* castaways is one by George Morland entitled 'African Hospitality': a romantic representation of the immediate aftermath of the wreck. In the background we see the dying vessel. Placed centre foreground we have the Hosea family with William, the father, hunched on his knees, looking upward at the face of an African warrior who stands over him. The warrior's arms are outstretched and his hands are open, gesturing towards a shelter. He is offering no threat, only compassion. All is well with the castaways, the painting tells us. They have fallen amongst what Victorian writers would later call 'Noble Savages'.

The following morning the demons of the night seemed to have disappeared. The moaning of the wounded did not sound so bad and the men were able to study their surroundings. A roll call revealed 15 dead. Logie, the Chief Mate, had collapsed into feverish unconsciousness and with neither instruments nor remedies there was little that the surgeon, Nixon, could do to help him or others in need.

There were 125 castaways in all: 91 seamen (including the captain and 5 officers, 8 servants, and 20 Petty Officers and artisans) and a total of 34 passengers. Lydia Logie, the Chief Mate's wife of eight months and now visibly pregnant, had ventured around the world to meet her mate and she watched as the life was now draining out of him, bathed in the sweats of dysentery or, as they called it in those days, 'the seaman's bloody flux'. William and Mary Hosea clung together with their young child Frances, with William still clutching the valuable package of diamonds. Everybody's fate now rested in the hands of one man, Captain John Coxon, but he appeared overwhelmed by the weight of his responsibilities.

Alexander Selkirk, history's best known castaway, landed on Juan Fernandez Island in 1704, some 80 years previously, but he had possessed a pistol and gunpowder, a hatchet and knife, some provisions and a pot for cooking. With these, and navigational instruments and charts, he survived five years before being rescued. The *Grosvenor* castaways had virtually nothing.

Now some decisions had to be made. Coxon knew that the Portuguese were at Delagoa Bay to the north and the Dutch were to the south. But in which direction should they go? Should they trek to the Portuguese or Dutch outpost, or stay put and deploy the skills of the artisan crew – carpenters, caulkers and coopers – to build another vessel? If they chose to strike out, should they stick to the shoreline and live off limpets and mussels, or venture inland, travelling more directly perhaps, but with the risk of attack from local tribes? The decision was made to head south along the beach. However, it was at Waterfall Bluff that they encountered their first challenge – the local tribe relieving the crew of the six cutlasses they possessed. (I am convinced that if one knew those people intimately, there would still be some of those cutlasses to be re-discovered.)

Many ships had been wrecked upon that stretch of coastline and it is no wonder that it is called the Wild Coast. Diaz, on his triumphant return to Lisbon, called the gateway to the Indies the Cabo de Todos los Tormentos – The Cape of All Storms.

Further down the coast they stumbled upon the present-day coastal resort of Mbotji. It was there that a supposedly demented Joshua Glover left the party and went off with the Pondo people. He privately told a seaman, Hynes, that he might as well die amongst the natives as starve on the beach.

Also at Mbotji, a man of a lighter skin with straight, silky black hair approached the castaways. He addressed Coxon in Dutch, which one John Sussman, who knew the language, translated. The man was a Javanese slave of the Dutch who had escaped up the coast, beyond the colonists' reach, and established a fiefdom among the Pondo. His advice to the senior men was unequivocal: a journey inland by such a party, including women and children, was quite impossible. They would have to pass through some of the densest forests in southern Africa, face possible attack by man and wild animal, cross numerous rivers and even traverse a desert to reach their destination.

Coxon offered the man a reward to act as their guide. He refused, saying that the Dutch would kill him on his return and that he also had a wife and children to look after. It was clear that he wanted nothing to do with the doomed enterprise. His parting words, as he hurried northward to plunder what was left of the wreck, were that they should hold to the coast, for if they ventured inland they would encounter Bushmen and Hottentots who would kill them all.

Lydia Logie, carrying an unborn child, was now having difficulty getting along and little Frances Hosea, just past her second birthday, bewildered and frightened, was crying as she stumbled on. An Italian seaman, Dominico Ciranio, picked up the weeping child and began to carry her. A second Italian, a portly man named Nardini, lay down and announced that he could go no further. This is how castaway parties start to split up and Nardini was the first to be abandoned.

On August 22, the party divided – one group headed for the interior, the other held to the coastline. At the mouth of the Umtata River, Captain Coxon, in the coastal group, plunged into the waters with a rope and was seen no more. The others somehow managed to make it across by raft. They carried on towards the Kei River. It is here that William Hosea, in a delirious state, dumped the parcel of diamonds. The abandoned gems were to resurface many years later, bringing neither fame nor fortune to their finder. Here's how this happened:

It was in 1925 when an elderly drifter, Johan Bock, found a bright stone on a farm that he had leased near the mouth of the Kei. Bock registered prospecting rights and other prospectors followed, paying Bock a concession right to explore. A Johannesburg mining inspector investigated the site and his suspicions were aroused. By the time the police descended on Bock's farm he had a cache of 1038 diamonds. Bock claimed they'd come from a cattle footpath but he was brought to court and charged with salting, or fraudulently placing, uncut gems for illegal gain. He was sentenced to three years hard labour. However, the court had ignored a key aspect of Bock's defence. Geological experts said that the diamonds were alluvial and could not have originated in South Africa. It was only in later years that sufficient evidence was found to exonerate Bock – he had actually discovered William Hosea's diamonds, deposited 137 years earlier. Of all the many stories associated with the fated vessel surely this must lay claim to being the most bizarre.

The first of the *Grosvenor* castaways arrived at Ferreira's Camp in Algoa Bay on 29 November 1782, after three months of walking more than 400 km from Lambasi Bay in Pondoland. The rumours started to spread soon after their arrival, including one regarding a white woman living with the Pondos. So strong were these rumours that two search parties were sent up the coast from Cape Town. The first party, of 1783, reached just past the Umtata River. The second, in 1791, went to the kraal just short of the Umzimvubu River, now called Port St. John's, and was lead by one Van Reenen. He wrote that they found three old women there who were willing to go back to the Cape, but insisted on taking their entire extended families with them. This being unfeasible, Van Reenen returned to the Cape. In the meantime, two of the servant women who had survived the journey were placed on a vessel bound for India. Two days into sailing, their ship was wrecked off Cape Agulhas and only one survived. The remainder of the survivors were shipped to England.

Other rumours persisted, one claiming that imprisoned women were being held in prostitution by black savages, though this was entirely untrue. There had been two men, found by the second search party, who had chosen to live with the Amapondo. They had taken wives and lived in harmony with the local people and refused to go back to the Cape. Another legend spoke of a white seven-year-old girl who had been rescued by the Amapondo. She was called Bessie, but the tribe had given her the name nGuma – 'the roar of the sea'. She later married the tribal chief and went on to reign over the Ama Tshomani tribe. The remnants of the Ama Tshomani still live in the area around Port St Johns – I wonder how many know the real story.

Shipwrecks have always fascinated people and the idea that sunken treasure exists is particularly compelling. The *Grosvenor* was no exception. There were numerous fraudsters who set about gathering investors' money to find the alleged wealth of the British East Indiaman. One of the best was Martin Luther Webster (I must add, no relation) and his Grosvenor Bullion Syndicate. Webster produced an archive of documents and maps that were supposedly from India. These included a bill of lading and an extract from Captain Coxon's logbook. The simple fact that these two documents would have been lying under the sea did not appear to deter the investors! The treasure, 'stored in the strong room beneath my cabin, along with 2 000 bars of gold and silver, stored in the bottom of the lazaretto', was said to have a value, in 1792, of no less than £1 714 710.

People flocked from around the world to subscribe for the 700 shares at a shilling a share, including such luminaries as Sir Arthur Conan Doyle (of Sherlock Holmes fame) – certainly no stranger to woolly stories! The reports back came thick and fast – 'the underground tunnel was only 150 ft from the hull now' – and the share price rocketed. Then, alas, silence. The *Rand Daily Mail* smelt a rat and an on-site inspection revealed that the tunnel was no more than a hole in the ground and the winch that had been paid for – which still lies there to this day – was rusting away.

This revelation should have sunk the entire fraud. However, interest was revived when a rival newspaper ran a story saying that the *Grosvenor* had been carrying the two Peacock Thrones, looted from Delhi, which were worth upwards of £5 million. The truth of the matter is, of course that the Peacock Thrones had been smashed by the Persian conqueror Nadir Shah when he sacked Delhi in 1739.

Finally the penny dropped, but not before the investors had lost their money.

It was not until early in 1982, a full 200 years after that disaster, that a Cape Town diver, Steve Valentine, was told by an excited friend that a single gold coin had been found at Lambasi Bay, now called Port Grosvenor. Steve decided to try the site, 600 m north of the Tezani River outlet. Many people have a vision that treasure diving involves finding wooden hulls on sandy sea beds – but nothing could be further from the truth. Steve said it was the most treacherous water and the roughest wreck he had ever dived in his life. The only thing that Valentine could see below the sea's surface was a blizzard of churning sand and bubbles.

But it was here that he struck gold – literally. On his first day's diving he brought to the surface material that, when separated, revealed star pagodas and ducats. The most intriguing item, however, was a silver buckle engraved with the initials 'CN'. There had been a passenger on board by the name of Charles Newman – one of the ill-fated individuals who had boarded the doomed vessel almost 200 years before.

The Magabeng – Part I
The story after creation

Bushmen paintings depict every aspect of the lives of Bushmen – their beliefs, fears, joys and, ultimately, their heartache. Because right up until the 1950s there were still Bushmen living in the Blaauberg region of the North West Province. They are there no more, but these ancient, gentle people live on through their extraordinary art.

Scattered amongst the Bushman art of the region are examples of 'Late-white art', a term used to describe the rock paintings of the Northern Sotho. These people, like the Bushmen, used the smooth sandstone surfaces of their shelters to depict their life-histories, myths and legends. I visited one of these underground galleries and was confronted by an astonishing image: a painting of a four-legged beast with an immense tongue that zigzags down to its feet and then three times the length of its body along the ground. The story behind this extraordinary picture was told to me by a man called Nwako Jonas Tlou Amma and what a story it is.

The painting is of the monster Kgolomodumo – 'the low rumbling noise' – who lived near Thaba Nanthlana –'the mountain that looks like the tip of a little spear'. Kgolomodumo had devoured all the animals and human beings on Earth. Only one pregnant woman, accompanied by two white doves, had managed to escape and find sanctuary in a cave. The doves fed the women during pregnancy until, in time, she gave birth to a little boy. She called him Mos An Yana Sen Kat Ana. When he grew older, the boy asked his mother why they never saw any other people and why he didn't have a father. She told him how Kgolomodumo had eaten all the people and animals. Mos An Yana Sen Kat Ana vowed that, when he reached manhood, he would slay the monster.

That day duly arrived. Mos An Yana Sen Kat Ana took his spear, shield, knife and axe and set off from the cave. On the way, he passed the two white doves that he had known from birth.

'Mos An Yana.' they called, 'if you give us some millet, we will give you advice on how to slay the monster.'

The young man lay millet on the ground and sat down to wait. The birds ate the grain, then said, 'Go and cut down some branches and sharpen them into staves. Then go down to the river and seek the tip of the monster's tongue in the water. Drive a stake through its tongue and pin it to the ground.'

Mos An Yana followed the birds' instructions. Coming upon Kgolomodumo at the river he drove a stake through the monster's tongue, so pinning it to the ground. He followed the tongue, staking it all the way up the monster's length to secure it. Plunging his spear into its belly he heard a voice cry out – 'Ouch!' He was startled; the people inside the monster were still alive! Going to another part of the creature, he poked his spear again and heard the buzzing of bees. Mos An Yana kept on probing until he arrived at a spot from where no sound came and there he cut open the carcass. All the people, animals and insects were released from the belly of the slain Kgolomodumo.

The following week the people elected Mos An Yana Sen Kat Ana as their chief. However, there were some who said that no normal mortal could have killed the powerful monster. These disbelievers said Mos An Yana must be a wizard and therefore put to death. They dragged Mos An Yana up the mountain to throw him off the sacred cliff. As they ascended the clouds started to gather, thicker and blacker than ever witnessed before. It became so dark that nothing could be seen and nobody moved, for fear of falling. The people were terrified. After a while, the clouds lifted and Mos An Yana Sen Kat Ana was nowhere to be seen. His ancestors had spirited away him.

What an incredible story, painting and people! I walked away from that rock shelter far in the Magabeng feeling I'd listened to the African version of Pandora's Box and wondering what other marvellous tales these ancient people have to tell us.

The Magabeng – Part 2

Frontier art in the Blaauberg

The Magabeng, that magical land in the west of the North West Province, is renowned for its Bushman art. The area of Blaauberg contains many fine examples of this wonderful rock art. But before I tell you about one astonishing painting there, it is imperative that you know just a little of the region's history.

The Bahananoa tribe used to live in this part of the country, under the able chieftainship of Malaboch. The sub-tropical Blaauberg, with its misty rains, ancient indigenous foliage and precipitous cliffs, is an inaccessible place. The Bahananoa lived high up in these mountains and through many years of practice could jump, skip and dance over the rocks, adapting remarkably well to this challenging environment.

When the British annexed the Transvaal in 1876 the Bahananoa had no gripe with them and agreed to pay their taxes. But when the ZAR took over from the British in 1881, Malaboch, who did not like and distrusted the Boers, refused to pay taxes to them. The missionaries there, Herbst and Sonntag, could see that this situation was only leading one way. The Berlin Missionary Station was under a man called Stech, who claimed that the missionary land belonged to the Missionary Station. When Stech was replaced by Herbst and the new missionary sent a blanket as a gift to Malaboch, the chief replied, 'I am afraid to accept this gift, because the teacher Stech said that the land on which the Mission Station stood belonged to him. Where he could have got this land from I do not know. If I should accept this gift, it will be said – now the new teacher has bought this land.' The offering was declined – an ominous sign.

The Native Commissioner stationed at Pietersburg, Vorster, was the government representative for the Southpans district. Arriving with eight Boers, he drove 100 head of Bahananoa cattle away. 'The Boers are looking for a pretext for war against us,' said the Chief.

From the to-ing and fro-ing of the negotiations, one can clearly see that the ZAR had decided to subjugate the local people. The plot became more complicated when minor chiefs like Matlala and Kibi, who wanted to oust Malaboch and seize power for themselves, sided with the Boers. By April 1894, the scene was set for war. Trainloads of troops disembarked at the railhead at Pietersburg, mounted their horses and headed for the Blaauberg. The Transvaal Staats Artillery with its Maxim and field guns, the Middelberg Commando and the Rustenberg Commando were included in those that came, all under the leadership of Commandant Piet Joubert. The artillery bombarded deep into the mountain strongholds where the Bahananoa were holed up. Unable to penetrate the fortresses in this way, the Boers destroyed the millet and grain crops on the surrounding plains and set to starve them out. The South African version of Masada was fully under way.

However, the Boers had not counted on a protracted war. As the conflict wore on they defected, taking about 20 000 head of cattle – which they claimed as booty – back to their farms. Paul Kruger was, therefore, forced to recruit the dregs of human society from the bars and the streets of Pretoria to prop up his 'army'. They proceeded to starve the Bahananoa out of the Blaauberg. When the Chief surrendered to save the last remnants of his dying people, they led him down the mountain with a rope around his neck then imprisoned him without a proper trial for six years. After the British re-occupied the Transvaal, in the Anglo-Boer War of 1900, Malaboch was set free and returned to his people.

This conflict is depicted in an astonishing painting, 12 m long, in a rock shelter in Blaauberg. A Bahananoa survivor of the battle is the artist. It starts on the top right-hand side with a train steaming into Pietersburg full of troops. Next, we see them de-training with their horses and riding up on commando. The scene that follows shows the bloody battle with Bahananoa warriors lying dead on the ground. The Boers are painted in aggressive stances with hats on their heads and guns and rifles in their hands, like cowboys in the Wild West. The sequence continues with a tableau illustrating the warriors being led away, their hands tied, to another train pointing in the opposite direction. Then you witness the tribesmen being transported by train to Pretoria. The very final scene of this unbelievable painting has the tribesmen being led off to the Pretoria jail under the armed guard of the Boers. I could picture the artist with tears running down his face as he recorded, for future generations, the terrible tragedy that had befallen his people.

I was awestruck: the whole Malaboch war was before my very eyes. I hung my head in desperate shame when I realised what had been done in the name of 'civilisation'. It is a marvellous, though troubling, work of art. Troubling, because it reminds one of the old familiar feelings of fear, loathing and hatred; feelings that we in the new South Africa have to put behind us as we try to heal the deep wounds of the past.

Constance Vivian

I have spent many years researching the stories of people who made the history of our country as rich and remarkable as it is. Some of these stories, mainly because of the characters involved, and what they got up to, stand head and shoulders above the others. The story I am going to relate is one of these.

Pilgrim's Rest and its gold miners are a long-forgotten part of history. Among the characters that arrived there, all seemingly larger than life, was a Negro pugilist known as 'Hobo Duck', who fought a stirring battle against Peter Gibbons and eventually married Agnes, the maid of Constance Vivian, who is the heroine of this story. There was 'Spanish Joe' whose total knowledge of the Spanish language was one sentence. There was Johannes Muller, who made a fortune up in the mountains and gave it all away to a kindly middle-aged woman who had nursed him back from death's door. Then there was the German, Baron Glüber, who used to teach the miners to sing *lieder*, and many, many more eccentric characters, including one Maria Espach, who was the only woman ever to be awarded the Burgers Cross medal.

Constance Vivian (alias 'Nonnie') was born in Exeter in Devonshire, and she held digging licence No. 661. She panned gold on her claim and made a great deal of money from it, for she was an astute businesswoman. It was at Pilgrim's Rest – the Valley of the Brutes, as she called it – that Constance found success, happiness and, alas, tragedy.

This is Nonnie's story. It goes back to one October day in 1874 when João Rodriques tied up his little boat at the jetty of what is now Maputo (a Mozambican port), which was then little more than a muddy hellhole. João Rodriques had made a tidy sum transporting his passengers some

450 kilometres up the coast from Port Natal (Durban). They were bound for the new gold diggings at Pilgrim's Rest and, despite being warned about the health risks in crossing the swamps between Maputo and the new-found gold fields, they insisted on taking the shortest route in order to obtain good claims. While the overland route was much safer, they could not spare the time.

It was a motley crew that ventured forth. There was a former lay preacher (now just as foulmouthed as the rest), a gold digger from the Yukon, a couple of deserters from deep-sea ships anchored in Port Natal's harbour, two young Englishmen out to see the world, and a forty-niner named Hugh Evans from San Francisco. The man appointed to lead them was one Gerald Venter. He was older than the others, a brawny man with a square chin who would brook no nonsense.

Each man chipped in five pounds, and Venter and Albright (one of the Englishmen) set off to buy a wagon and supplies, while the rest set up camp. Their purchases included 'Dr Livingstone's', the only 'medicine' known for swamp fever. It was a mixture of jalap, chamomile, rhubarb and quinine, and, if it did not bring the fever under control within 24 hours, the patient would, in all probability, die. Venter and Albright met up with a man named John Vivian who had come down from Nyasaland (now Malawi) and was about to set off for Pilgrim's Rest with his daughter Constance. He had already acquired a wagon with a span of oxen. John Vivian invited Venter's party to join him and Nonnie on the trek. He said he would not charge them for their share in the long journey on two conditions. They would have to buy their own horses and provisions for the long journey and nobody was to come near Nonnie, who had a very large protector in the person of her maid, Agnes.

And so they all set off for the swamps. On the first night Nonnie pulled out a banjo, and they all sang around the campfire. The group had left a trifle too late in the year and the fever, which seemed to abate during winter, was at its worst during the rainy summer season, which had now begun! As they entered the swamps, they were overcome by the odour of decay. They had to cover some 270 kilometres in 9 days. After 76 kilometres, they would reach the foothills of the Lebombos; after 96 kilometres, the

Portuguese-controlled border; 124 kilometres, the Komatie River; then the Crocodile, some 20 kilometres further.

One day, in the course of the journey, they stopped at a little village where they learned from the chief that there was a very sick white man lying in one of the huts. Venter entered the hut, and there, on a pile of blankets, lay a bearded old man who had been stricken by the fever. His name, as they discovered from his belongings after he died, was Herman Haupt and he had been a prospector. They buried him in the shade of a tree.

Later, Evans, who had found a bottle of brandy amongst Haupt's belongings, sat down to drink it in the bushes, within full view of Nonnie's bathing alcove. When Nonnie came out to bath, he made a run for her in her nakedness. As he grabbed her, she screamed, and Agnes – hearing the screams – came running. On seeing Evans pulling Nonnie to the ground, she lifted him up with her powerful arms and threw him with all her might. His head went through the spokes of the wagon wheel, his body carrying on past. There was a sharp crack as his neck broke, and Evans, the would-be rapist, was no more.

None of the other roughnecks attempted anything similar throughout the rest of the journey. John Vivian recorded what had happened, and the papers of the enquiry that was held later are now in the records of the Landdrost of Lydenburg of 1876 and filed in Pretoria.

The next night, Amos Drayer, the gold digger from the Yukon, refused his food and lay down to rest, looking tired and ill. Nonnie took his temperature – yes, it was the fever. They made him hot bush tea, to sweat it out, but by evening Drayer's temperature was 105 °F. James Clive had also begun to feel unwell and died the following evening, bringing the death toll on the trek to three. No one knew the cause of the fever at the time – the diggers thought that it came from the miasma arising from the rotting vegetation of the swamps. (The conqueror of malaria, Donald Ross, was still to have his day, and when he placed the blame on the true cause of the illness, the *Anopheles* mosquito, he was ridiculed.)

The party reached and crossed the Crocodile River without further incident. The Transvaal government had attempted, without success, to establish a rest station at the Crocodile River, but no one could be induced to stay anywhere between Pretoriuskop and the eastern ocean. The first man with sufficient experience to do so was Hart, who was shot on the threshold of his cabin, some 22 kilometres from Pretoriuskop, by a party of natives who had come to him to complain that a white man had robbed them of a rifle. The little station, including Hart's animals, had been burnt to the ground. When the Venter trek got there they found only burnt-out huts.

On the last leg of their journey, the group became very angry with Malika, the leader of their native crew, who had staggered back from a nearby village so drunk that he could hardly walk. Malika grabbed John Vivian by the arm and led him to where cattle were grazing. He staggered over to the nearest beast and pointed to the distended stomach. They had entered tsetse-fly country.

Having endured this difficult journey, John Vivian and his daughter and the group of like-minded travellers arrived at the newly discovered goldfields of Pilgrim's Rest. This was towards at the close of 1874. The town had just been nicknamed 'Mac-Mac' by Thomas Burgers, the President of the Republic, on account of all of the Scottish families digging for gold there. Mac-Mac was abuzz with people, some of whom were starting to become famous, such as Miss Espach, who warmly received John Vivian and his daughter.

Miss Espach had just been honoured by Thomas Burgers with the highly regarded Burgers Cross medal. This was in respect of her work as an unflinching nurse who had cared for wounded men during the Sekhukhune Wars.

There was a well-known man, named Muller, in that area who was a bit of a historian. Muller told the young diggers to beware of the 'gold fever' that, according to the old people, left any infected persons doomed forever. Some did strike it lucky – a certain man named Barnett had made £5 000 within four months, an absolute fortune in those days. But by far the vast majority of people in that area suffering from 'gold fever' died by the thousands and now lie in marked and unmarked graves scattered around the countryside. Muller told of how, once the nuggets in the Pilgrim's Rest area had been found, word spread like wildfire fanned by a strong wind and, as the smell of gold travelled, men began to converge on the valley. Some of the early arrivals had seen burnt-out kraals, and had heard that this had been the work of Ma Nthathisi, the black BaTlokwa Boudicca.

Another early arrival at Pilgrim's Rest was Spanish Joe. History would show that he would be one of the last to leave. He never spoke about his past until one night, full of hooch, he related how, as a young man, he had been left behind by his ship in Valencia, Spain. The good-looking young man related how, as a beachcomber, he had had several successful encounters with the local girls. On one such encounter, an angry Spanish father had chased him on horseback. Spanish Joe had had his hands tied together, and been made to run back to Valencia, behind the horse. There he had been thrown into gaol, spending a week without being charged, before being released. Joe was actually Italian and knew only one sentence in Spanish, 'Will you sleep with me?'

There were also many old people at Pilgrim's Rest. Some had come from Kimberley, deserting the diamond fields, others had come from farms around Grahamstown, and parts of the coast. The Natal route was very congested with travellers. In the little roadside inns, men slept in any and every corner they could find on their journey northwards to Pilgrim's Rest. At Newcastle, Natal, diggers returning with treasures from Pilgrim's Rest amazed the local people by spreading newspaper on hotels' billiard tables to display gold nuggets from the newly found gold-digging valley.

Nonnie's father, John, wanted to farm in the Lydenburg area, but Nonnie had other ideas. She wanted to stay. 'This is no place for a girl,' her father said, explaining that they as a family belonged to farming stock. 'We know nothing about gold digging.' It was then that he realised the worst – that his daughter had contracted gold fever. Muller assured John Vivian that although the work would be very laborious, his daughter would be in safe hands. Constance remained firm, saying that she was having nothing to do with her father's plans to farm in Lydenburg. Moving quickly, she went down to the Mining Commissioner's offices and paid 5 shillings, which afforded her claim 661. It was then that John Vivian realised he could do nothing to stop Nonnie.

Constance Vivian started working her claim almost immediately with the help of Agnes and some newly enlisted labourers. They first removed the boulders from the river with a crowbar. Following this hard labour they dug into the soft soils and put through a sluice for channelling the water from the river for sieving in order to obtain nuggets. The rest had to be panned for 'tailings'. It was backbreaking work. On the level bank, above the water's edge, Nonnie set up her white tent alongside all the other white tents up and down the river valley.

In the meantime, her father had decided that, gold or no gold, he would give her a couple of weeks, and then he would take her with him to Lydenburg. He was not having his only daughter living in a place where there was continual collusion between the hard-drinking diggers and the single policeman. He had quickly observed what a strange place Pilgrim's Rest was. For instance, when one of the prisoners got tired of his rations in gaol, he asked whether he could get a decent square meal at the hotel and he was permitted to do so! Furthermore, when this same prisoner returned to the lock-up, the policeman, in sulky tones, declined to let him in! He said that if the prison food was not good enough for him, then he should go elsewhere!

The characters in Pilgrim's Rest were a colourful lot. There was a university man named Fabian, the son of an English bishop. Fabian lived in a cave on the hillside. During his drinking bouts, which usually coincided with the arrival of the mail from England, he would sit up all night, quoting Greek plays, and, in the wee hours, roar out choruses from Sophocles's *Electra* and *Antigone*. One day, after a particularly heavy spell of drinking, he announced that he would never drink brandy again. This posed a problem, as he had just purchased a case of the stuff. In order to help the situation, the locals raffled the case, and the lucky winner was a man named Colquhoun. Few could pronounce the name, so they called him Connie.

Then there was one Herbert Rhodes, the little-known brother of Cecil John Rhodes. Herbert had participated in the founding of the De Beers diamond empire and he had heard that the Bapedi chief Sekhukhune had a cave full of diamonds from the earliest days of the Kimberley diggings.

Chief Sekhukhune had always been at loggerheads with President Burgers, for Burgers wanted Sekhukhune's land, and had tried to impose a hut tax, which Sekhukhune refused to pay. Sekhukhune desperately wanted a cannon or two, and offered a bucket of diamonds to anyone who could supply. Rhodes got in touch with Sekhukhune, and a deal was made.

The cannon in question was brought up the coast to Lourenço Marques in a small French ship, lowered over the side into a boat, and rowed up the Maputo River, to a predetermined meeting place. Unfortunately, during the voyage, Rhodes quarrelled with a man on board and gave him a sound thrashing. The man went ashore and told the Portuguese authorities all about the deal. As it was an unthinkable crime to sell guns to black chiefs in those days, they dispatched soldiers upstream to seize the gun and arrest Herbert Rhodes.

A friend of Rhodes overheard it all and sent a swift runner to inform Rhodes of the danger. Rhodes was as wily as a fox. He tied a rope around the cannon and string to the end of the rope. He then tied a piece of wood to the end of the string, and threw the cannon overboard, and sat there, confidently, waiting for the soldiers. Upon arrival, the officer arrested Rhodes, who protested his innocence and demanded an explanation of the outrage. When told of the gunrunning charge, he indignantly demanded that the officer produce the gun. Alas, no gun could be found. The officer was most apologetic; he knew that he was in trouble. At this stage Herbert Rhodes overplayed his hand, saying that the British government would be told of his arrest, and that a gunboat would be sent up from Simon's Town to blow the hell out Lourenço Marques!

Rhodes had forgotten one important thing – the Maputo River was tidal and the tide had been going out. One of the more astute soldiers had noticed something in the mud and called the Sergeant to investigate. Shortly afterwards, the cannon was hauled out and Herbert Rhodes and his party were frog-marched back to Lourenço Marques to be imprisoned in Fort Lydsaamheid.

Another character worth a mention was 'Harry the Sailor', whose real name was Arthur Augustus Bryant. He had been a sea captain in the square-riggers and commanded the *Flying Cloud*, which had plied the ocean between Bristol and Valparaiso. He ran aground with a cargo of sulphur on the sharp rocks of Wellington Island off the southwest coast of Chile. Bryant and two others got ashore, and spent six miserable months crossing the peninsula to Patagonia. He often told of how he became chief of a certain Indian tribe, and as such, exercised the rights of *droit de seigneur* over the girls of the tribe. But the intense cold and the raw spirits brewed by the Indians did not agree with him, and on getting to Santa Cruz he signed up as a deck hand, only to desert the ship at Cape Town and trek upcountry to the renowned gold fields. His time in the valley was brief; he left for Durban after he had dug out a 12-pound gold nugget.

Nonnie, with pick and shovel in hand, would join her labourers and wade into the river, digging for gold in the valley at Pilgrim's Rest. The gold diggers with claims around her had both made good strikes already and her time was running out. John Vivian was getting ready to proceed with his plans to go farming at Lydenburg. He was still going to take his daughter and, much against her wishes, her tent was packed up. She walked up to her friend Gerald Venter and said, 'I hope you make a million, Gerald, and I shall not forget you!' To which he replied, 'If you don't come back, I will come and fetch you!' She fell into a deep sadness, and, as they drew away, she turned in her saddle to look back across the beautiful valley, knowing that a portion of her very soul would always remain there.

After spending six months at her father's farm in Lydenburg, Nonnie left for a shopping visit in Pretoria, returning to the valley on her way. She sent word for Gerald Venter to meet her at the hotel. Gerald was overcome with the joy of seeing her again but refused her request to accompany her on the journey. He explained that he would have loved nothing more than to go, but could not do so because claim jumping had become so rife in the valley. Unattended claims would be jumped even if they were left for just a few days and Gerald Venter had been looking after Constance Vivian's claim for her on a daily basis. Nonnie realised that the kindly Gerald Venter was a man in a million, and that, on her return from Pretoria, she would be returning to where her heart lay and not to the farm in Lydenburg, as her father thought.

While in Pretoria, Nonnie got word that her father had fallen desperately ill, causing her to cut her visit short and hasten back to him. Finding him very ill indeed and in the care of the neighbours who had been nursing him while she was away, she decided that a complete change in climate was called for. Neither Lydenburg nor the rough-and-ready, dirty little town of Pilgrim's Rest – where she was still hoping to make her fortune – were fit places for John Vivian to recover his health. Wrapping him in blankets and putting him in the back of the spider cart, she set off for Durban. Before this, however, she sent the news to Gerald Venter.

The new hotel in Pilgrim's Rest was now completed and one day a coach arrived, watched by local spectators, including Gerald Venter. As the coach drew up he saw that the girl passengers were wondering how they were going to reach the ground level from their roof-top seats. Stepping forward, Gerald Venter caught one girl and then the next as they leapt from the coach to be lowered safely to the ground. The second, a merry-faced, nose-tilted girl, with red hair, threw her arms around him and kissed him as she slid to the ground. As Venter laughed, she said, 'I hope I'll be seeing you soon, then I can thank you properly.' Nonnie had witnessed this incident and explained to the naïve Gerald Venter that these were the *filles de joie* arriving at Pilgrim's Rest and they both had a good laugh.

Such was the backdrop to the hard and harsh world of the early town where Nonnie Vivian had already accumulated from her claim a total of £60 000.

We now take up the story when Constance Vivian, after consulting a doctor at Wakkerstroom, travels with her father by post coach to Natal. She witnesses the Dutch farmers trekking northwards out of Natal away from the British, for the new Republic of Natalia had now been disbanded. The old Zulu Chief Mpande had recently died and Cetshwayo had taken over. This new British presence left the Zulus uneasy and restless. It would be another four years before the British army, in 1879, crossed the Nyati River in a campaign to destroy the might of the Zulus forever, culminating in the bloody battle of Ulundi and the seizure of Zululand by Britain.

On arrival in Durban, Constance Vivian rented a house on the Berea for her ailing father's convalescence. She found herself in the midst of a society far removed from the harshness of the buckets and picks, drunkards and prostitutes of those gold fields of Pilgrim's Rest. Gerald Venter followed soon after to claim his bride. Now dressed in the frippery of Durban society, Nonnie for the first time admired this gentle man who thus far she had called her friend. Around the dining-room table – she in all of her finery and he, for the first time, in a magnificent dark suit – she realised that this was the man for her. With a little persuasion from her father, they called upon the services of Reverend Greaves and arranged to have the banns called for the next three successive Sundays. For the afternoon of their marriage her father had booked a single cabin on a ship departing for Cape Town for their honeymoon. It was during this honeymoon that one Henry Edwards drew the only known likeness of Constance or Nonnie Vivian, now Mrs Gerald Venter. It is the only likeness of this brave lady that survives to this day.

The honeymooners were blissfully happy. But both of them, being used to the active and hard outdoor life of the diggings of Pilgrim's Rest, soon tired of the mundane society of Cape Town. Within a week they had booked their passage back to the world that they knew so well. At the end of their return journey they found that Nonnie's beloved father, John Vivian, had passed away. They did what had to be done and then went back to Pilgrim's Rest.

Nonnie had a brilliant idea that culminated in them registering a new claim further downstream and away from the river. MacDonald, the mining commissioner, laughed, saying that they wouldn't find gold there. They did, and plenty of it. Nonnie fell pregnant and had a son and things were very pleasant for the Venter family. But fate somehow just seems to change the course of life as soon as happiness, prosperity and love are found. It happened that Gerald and a friend were travelling on horseback to Lydenburg and had to pull over to allow a commando to pass. It was the start of the First Boer War just before 1880. Gerald was deeply troubled. He had no axe to grind with the English, and yet in his heart he knew he was a Boer. On the return journey, they saw another commando, and

Gerald slipped from the saddle, shook his friend's hand, and asked him to explain to Nonnie what he had to do. He then turned and walked over to join the Boer commando. He was welcomed and they started riding south towards the Majuba border of Natal and the Transvaal, between Volksrust and Newcastle.

The British, who were garrisoned at Lydenburg under Lieutenant-Colonel Anstruther, had received instructions to muster their forces and relieve Pretoria. Packing up and leaving was a lengthy affair. There were wagons to be bought and parties to say farewell to all the ladies. All in all, it took Anstruther's so-called Flying Column a full three weeks to depart, which they finally did to the sounds of the band that led them away playing 'Kiss me, Mother, kiss your darling'. The Flying Column made about ten miles a day, and were ambushed and shot to ribbons by the Boers on the banks of the Bronkhorstspruit River, where Anstruther died, and the 94th Regiment of foot soldiers was no more.

On the Natal side of Majuba Hill, were the forces of General Pomeroy Colley. On the Transvaal side of the hill lay the Boer troops, and to cut a whole battle short, the English captured the hill in February of 1881. The Boers stormed it the following day from the base; up and up they climbed, hidden by the smoke of their rifles, as fusillade after fusillade came down from the crest of the hill. It was difficult for the British to hit individuals through that smoke, but one person, Gerald Venter, was hit. He lay dead on the side of Majuba Hill.

Back home, Nonnie received two letters: one from Gerald in which he told her of his decision to go and fight, and the second from Commandant Slabber, telling her of Gerald's untimely death. Hers was not the only grieving soul, for back home in England, General Pomeroy Colley's wife received a letter her late husband had written to kiss her good night. He had a bullet through his heart when found the following day.

Nonnie was destroyed; she wandered around the house in a vacant stupor, not being able to grasp the fact that never again would Gerald rush into the room and pick his son up from the cot. Never again would she feel his touch. To her, the laughter of that valley – Pilgrim's Rest – coupled with the fact that two thirds of the original diggers had already left, put her in the depths of depression. The gods are so cruel. Her bonny boy, who was laughing at lunchtime, went into convulsions and was dead before midnight. Nonnie Venter now had nothing. She decided to move to Cape Town, putting her house on the market. There were no buyers in the valley now as the companies were taking over. She had the house boarded up and took the coach to the coast.

On the way, she visited the field where her beloved Gerald had been buried. She was in a terrible way, a woman so destroyed by grief that she had no more tears left to cry. She had received a letter from Agnes, her former maid, who had married Hobo Duck. After the marriage, they had left for Louisiana and Agnes now wrote about how they hated the United States and desperately wanted to come home. Nonnie sent them money for their immediate passage to Cape Town. She built a home in Tamboerskloof and there Hobo Duck found a job at the Star Fisheries, and Agnes went back to the old days with her darling Nonnie. Hobo came home one day having been fired for not speaking Afrikaans among the coloureds in Cape Town. Nonnie, who was incensed, told Hobo to rein the horses and the cart so that she could go and speak to the owner of the company. She was shown into the owner's office and was shattered when she found the man who had wanted to court her at Pilgrim's Rest, one Arthur Summerville, otherwise known as Piper. When he was in his cups in the old days, he used to take out his bagpipes, and the valley would be filled with the screeches of the Scottish demons, until he either passed out or somebody threatened to kill him. Hobo was immediately reinstated. Over a long period of time, having shared their grief, Nonnie and Piper decided to marry, for they had a lot in common and made good companions.

Nonnie often wanted to revisit the memories of her past life, but Arthur begged her not to reopen old wounds. She was, however, a hard-headed woman. They first travelled up to Pretoria, where Nonnie was overcome by terrible pains in her chest; Arthur was beside himself, and after a thorough examination, the doctor confirmed she was not suffering from indigestion, but rather that her heart was taking serious strain. She asked Arthur to take her to Pilgrim's Rest and he obliged. They found the valley deserted, the hotel closed, none of the rowdy pubs full of friends drinking to celebrate a find. The companies had taken over and if there was a good find, a small bonus was paid to the individual, certainly not enough to entertain friends. Arthur tore the planks off the front door of Nonnie's home, and walked into town to get provisions for the evening meal. Feeling alone and scared, Nonnie touched her old things and remembered times gone by. Very soon her eyes fell upon the vacant cot and she fell down, sobbing ceaselessly. When Arthur returned from the village he was going to insist that they leave as soon as it was light. Searching for Nonnie, he walked through to the child's room. Her body was still warm, but, in reliving the memories, her heart had given in and she was gone.

Tearing off his coat, he left the house to find the cairn where he had buried his bagpipes. He played those damaged reeds until they would produce no more sound that night. The only person still remaining from they heyday of Pilgrim's Rest was Spanish Joe, in a drunken stupor. When he heard the screech of those pipes he stirred and said, 'My God – if I hadn't known better, I would have sworn that that was Piper Summerville.'

Following Nonnie's death, her sister-in-law, Mrs Blackburn, claimed her Durban house on the Berea. It is not known who got the Cape Town property; all that is known is that it was used after her death by the staff of a nearby nursing home.

The missionary station of Genadendal – or the Valley of Mercies

One of the most successful Governors of the Cape Colony was Hendrik Swellengrebel. He was the first South-African born Governor of the Cape, the son of a Russian named Jan Swellengrebel and a local-born lass called Johanna Krysa. He joined the Dutch East India Company at a young age, rose to the position of Second in Command by 1737, and was elevated to the Governorship of the Cape in 1739. He was one of the Cape's most resourceful Governors and a staunch advocate of agriculture, opening up many new farming areas, one of which still bears his name to this day: Swellendam.

The Dutch Reformed Church was up in arms when Hendrik permitted the Moravians to open up a mission station for the Hottentots in the interior, at a spot first known as Baviaanspoort but later renamed Genadendal, or the Valley of Mercies. General Janssens renamed it again in 1806 and the little town of Jansenville, south of Graaff-Reinet, still bears his name.

The Mission Station was originally set up by a George Schmidt to convert the Hottentot and African 'heathen' to Christianity. Schmidt pitched his tent in the valley know as Baviaanskloof, a beautiful place in the cleft of the mountains watered by a perennial stream. He was a remarkably humble missionary and it was not long before a large number of the local tribes, as well as the remnants of the Bushmen, gathered around him. But, as is nearly always the case, the person who sets out to do a good job attracts too much attention and is inevitably overtaken by politics.

The Dutch Reformed Church informed Schmidt that he was taking too much upon himself, that he should have limited his zeal to the conversion of the 'heathens' and that he should not have taken it upon himself to baptise these people, but taken them instead to the nearest 'predikant' for baptism.

And so it was that a Council of Policy appointed three Dutch Reformed ministers to look into the matter. They pronounced Schmidt's conduct contrary to the law and recommended that a Dutch missionary should be sent from Holland to minister the community at Genadendal. 'All this', Schmidt said stoutly, 'is very absurd.' But to take on the formidable Dutch Reformed Church was impossible. The Church branded him a heretic and his community, further displaced by the impact of neighbouring farmers, fell to pieces. And so it was that George Schmidt, the man with the big heart, returned to Europe with his spirit broken and his work at the once beautiful Moravian Mission Station at an end.

Time and again the Moravian Society sought permission to send men out to carry on the work; time and again it was denied. Eventually, in November 1792, a full fifty years after the sorrowful departure of George Schmidt, permission was obtained from the Governor of the Cape to continue the good work at Genadendal.

Murder most foul

Paarl, the beautiful gem village of the Cape, contains an old 'pastorie' of the Dutch Reformed Church, which nowadays houses the Huguenot Museum. And, if you know where to look, tucked away in a forgotten old storeroom lies a slate gravestone with a skull and crossbones at its crescent. It is the gravestone of one J W L Gebhart jnr, aged 22, who died on 15 November 1822. He was convicted of murder and hanged.

The legend surrounding the tragic death of this young man was fleshed out years ago, and passed down from generation to generation.

The story starts in Holland where a *raadsheer* was troubled by the imminent birth of an illegitimate son, of whom he was the father. He persuaded a church schoolmaster, one J W L Gebhart, to marry the girl. Gebhart, by way of reward, was appointed Dutch Reformed minister for Paarl in the faraway Cape of Good Hope. He was also entrusted with 10 000 guilders for the child's education. If the child died, Gebhart could keep the money, but if the boy reached maturity the balance belonged to the young man.

In the pastorie just mentioned the wife gave birth to a boy. They called him Johan Wilhelm Ludwig, after the minister. The wife died shortly afterwards. The dominee then married Johanna du Toit, the daughter of the manager of the pastorie farm, who bore him two sons and a daughter – it was always said that Gebhart favoured these three over Wilhelm.

Wilhelm grew into a quiet, hardworking lad, who served the minister well on the family farm in the Klapmuts area. At the age of 21 he fell in love with the daughter of a church *ouderling*, a girl called Martjie.

Then, one day, a slave named Klaas gave trouble and the minister ordered Wilhelm to thrash him. The softhearted Wilhelm had no stomach for this but did as his father ordered, punishing Klaas as four other slaves held him down. That same night he told his stepmother that he'd objected to what had been asked of him and had resolved to leave the farm the following morning. Early the next day, Wilhelm left. When the slaves were called to work, Klaas was missing. A search located Klaas – lying dead in the slaves' quarters.

The minister found Wilhelm, whom he denounced. A Dr Barneveldt certified that the slave had died as the result of a beating. Young Wilhelm was arrested and appeared before the Landrost at Stellenbosch. Minister Gebhart gave evidence against him, declaring that he had beaten the slave mercilessly. Wilhelm was tried before the High Court in Cape Town and sentenced to death. The court records state that this was such a crushing blow for the young man that he could neither eat nor drink.

Martjie's father, the church *ouderling*, went to tell Wilhelm about the *raadsheer* and the legacy. He explained that the *raadsheer* had written to him, as an elder of the church, setting out the facts and had asked him to find out whether the money had been paid over. Of course, the money had never been transferred to him. Wilhelm then understood why it was that his father had always hated him. The *ouderling* went on to tell Wilhelm that there was a strong suspicion, as yet unproven, that his stepfather had made another slave beat Klaas to death that night. The slaves were all, quite naturally, afraid to speak out.

'My poor boy,' the *ouderling* said, 'I have done everything in my power, but there is no hope of securing a reprieve. I have written to the *raadsheer*, revealing all, but when the reply comes it will be too late.'

Wilhelm took the ring from his finger and said, 'Give this to Martjie. Tell her that, in the eyes of the world, I die a murderer, but in the eyes of God, a martyr.'

On Friday, 5 November 1822, as young Gebhart stood on the trapdoor, he turned and said, 'We are all weak and sinful humans, but I do not die as a murderer. I forgive all my persecutors and all who gave evidence against me. I die in peace.'

Wilhelm was buried between the two big trees in his stepmother's garden, just as he'd requested. Dr Barneveldt committed suicide shortly after the event. The slave that was instructed to beat Klaas that night went to the Landrost to confess, but because the Landrost and other officials were scared of being accused of an unjust hanging, he was turned out of the offices. The following week the slave hanged himself in one of the trees by Wilhelm's grave.

Such is the story of the gravestone in the Huguenot Museum. Translated from the Dutch it reads:

'Rest in peace unhappy youth
Your career was short and beset
  With a false path of temptation
There is little joy in this world
  And much suffering

'By his faithful broken-hearted
Brother and Aunt
Henry Gebhart and
Johanna Wolf (Born Gebhart)'

The Eastern Cape

What strikes me most about the people of the Eastern Cape is their warm, open nature and generous hospitality. There is an earthiness amongst those people that I am sure originates from some of their ancestors – the 1820 Settlers.

Take the little town of Humansdorp. When I was searching for the grave of Hendrik Spoorbek (whom I have written about previously) – the old *towenaar* who in the early 1900s eked out a living by casting protective spells on the thatched roofs of farmers' dwellings and barns – all I knew was that he was buried on the banks of a dam on the Krom River. My wife thought we had no chance of finding him. We visited the local police station and told a constable what we were looking for.

'I know that name,' said the policeman, 'it was mentioned with the 100 year celebration of Humansdorp, but there is only one dam on the Krom River and that is the Churchill Dam up near Kareedouw. If you wait 15 minutes while I finish up, I'll take you personally.'

At the Churchill Dam we met the manager of the Port Elizabeth Municipal Water Works. He had spent 15 years studying Hendrik Spoorbek the Towenaar. He had photographs of his house's foundations, taken when the dam was very low, and he knew where his grave was. What a find! But such are the rewards of getting to know the peoples of my country.

Now consider the lovely city of Port Elizabeth; it is no wonder that it is called the 'friendly city'. It is a place where people bend over backwards to help you. A group of us were there to capture on film the only monument erected to that enigmatic character, the elusive Prester John. Port Elizabeth also holds the sole monument to be erected in remembrance of the millions of horses that fell during the Anglo-Boer and First World wars. The place and its people have heart and passion. (Incidentally, the museum there, run by Dr Jenny Benny, houses stunning examples of dinasours and ichthyology and also has an outstanding collection of maritime archaeology. It is well worth a visit when you're in the city.)

To give you some background to the city, there were originally Khoi tribes who lived here. They would bring their cattle down to the stream originally called Kragga Kamma, which in the Hottentot language means 'Stony Waters'. The name was later changed to the Baakens River. The Portuguese navigators originally called Algoa Bay 'Bahia De Lagoa' (The Bay of the Lagoon). In 1488, at a headland now known as Kwaai Hoek, they erected a pillar in honour of St. Gregory, hence the modern corruption – Cape Padrone. The remains of the pillar's cross stand in the Witwatersrand Library in Johannesburg. In August 1799, during a period of British occupation, a stone redoubt of 24 square metres overlooking the mouth of the Baakens River was constructed and named Fort Frederick, after the Duke of York.

It was Sir Rufane Donkin, the visiting Acting Governor of the Cape, who on 6 June 1799 named the town Port Elizabeth, in memory of his beloved wife. Elizabeth had died of fever in India two years previously, at the tender age of 28. Sir Rufane also built a stone pyramid honouring his wife – on the hill above the landing place at Algoa Bay. The monument with its moving inscription still stands in the Donkin Reserve.

Of course, Port Elizabeth is also well known for a terrible shipping disaster that occurred on 31 August 1902. There were 28 ships lying at anchor in the bay before the storm hit. After the destructive gale had subsided, 19 craft lay wrecked on the shoreline and only 9 could be seen in the bay.

No trip down to this neck of the woods would be complete without a brief visit to the little town of Alexandria, named after Reverend Alexander Smith, who ministered to the population in the 1840s. This is chicory and pineapple country, but if you know where to look you can still find the Mooi Meisies Saal, erected by the voortrekker Karel

Landman. This is where all the district people and townsfolk ran for shelter at the beginning of the Seventh Frontier War. The Xhosa were crazed – burning and looting the town. The townsmen were desperately defending their homes – shooting out of the windows while the women stood beside them, reloading the rifles. The Xhosa began to throw torches onto the grass roof, but it was Hendrik Spoorbeck who said, 'Don't worry folks – I put a spell on this roof and it won't burn.' The Xhosa eventually retreated under the heat of the withering fire, and, guess what? – the thatch of Mooi Meisies Saal didn't catch alight!

Such are the memories and legends of the wonderful Eastern Cape.

The oaks of the fair Cape

One of the most beautiful sights, to me, is the displays of ancient oak trees which are such a prevalent feature of the Cape landscape. Nowhere else in South Africa will you find so many Common Oaks, Pin Oaks and evergreen Holm Oaks, though the last variety does grow successfully in the Free State and Gauteng.

The Common Oak, whose history is outlined here, was first introduced by Jan van Riebeeck, though not in large numbers. Simon van der Stel, the Governor of the Cape, became the first oak planter of note. He understood the need for wind breaks in the region and, within five years, more than 5 000 acorn-bearing trees were planted, many of them in Stellenbosch. There were over 50 000 young oaks in the nursery at Rustenberg (near Rondebosch), ready to be sent to farmers and Landrosts, and during this period Constantia was also planted with oaks.

Van der Stel passed a law requiring all farmers to plant 100 oak trees every year. Although the farmers complained that the trees harboured birds that ate their crops, the Governor ensured that the law was enforced. He also planted 16 000 young and tender trees, the thickness of a finger, in the good soils above Groote Schuur and beyond. In a ten-year period most had achieved a height of 10 m.

When Willem Adriaan van der Stel succeeded his father as Governor he planted – before the end of the seventeenth century – a further 10 000 oaks in the peninsula, mostly in the Newlands area.

The ensuing Governors were not as energetic as these two, though a *placaat*, or rule, was passed forbidding damage to any trees on public property. Anyone flouting the law was subjected to the penalty of 'Being tied to the foot of the gallows, and publicly flogged'. Sometimes I feel that it is a pity that this law no longer stands!

This whole story begs the question, 'Where is the oldest oak in the Cape to be found?' From the skimpy information I have at my disposal, it is possibly the oak that lives beside the La Cotte homestead on the wine farm of the same name in the Franschhoek Valley. The family legend has it that a certain French Huguenot, Jean Gardiol, brought an acorn from France with him and planted it there in 1694. That makes the tree just over 310 years old. I know that 'Eikestad' or 'Oak Town', which is the old nickname for Stellenbosch, will desperately want to claim line honours in this regard but to my knowledge there is no record of an older oak.

Lady Anne Barnard mentions the beautiful oak-lined street of Stellenbosch. She sketched 'The Drostdy', showing the two oaks on either side that were planted in Simon van der Stel's time. A few years after Lady Anne's visit another traveller, by the name of Barrows, favourably compared the oaks to the largest elms in Hyde Park, London. This lady totally abhorred the fact that over 50 of these beautiful trees had been rooted out to raise a paltry sum of money for the local parish – the venerable giants lying in ruins on the streets.

Today, of course, the old trees are only removed when nothing can be done to ensure the safety of the general public. And Stellenbosch still has one street of oaks, Dorp Street, which runs from the old parsonage to the railway crossing. Every one of them is protected by the Historical Monuments Council.

Paarl, just after the Second World War, had to bid a sad farewell to an oak planted in Main Street in 1824 by a Mr J J Luttig, the *Koster* of the Dutch Reformed Church. This beauty had attained a height of about 30 m. When it became rotten the tree was sawn down and the local municipality provided a brass plaque detailing its history. Now that's showing caring and civilised behaviour.

My last point on the topic of oaks is that years ago many of the small hamlets and villages of the Cape would hold municipal acorn sales every autumn. The people would gather and bid for the right to collect acorns in the different streets. I know that Ceres (named after the Roman Goddess of Agriculture) continued this tradition for over sixty years. The children of the poorer families would gather the acorns and sell them to the local farmers at 10 shillings a bag, thereby earning up to two pounds a week.

The only trouble was that pigs with too many acorns in their diet are liable to yield a low-grade, bluish, oily bacon, so the farmers had to watch the quantities quite carefully.

Sometimes, in modern civilisation, where these quaint rites and rituals have fallen by the wayside, I cannot help but think that we are all the poorer for it.

The saddle

Om Mias was sitting under the shade of a peach tree, smoking. The sun beat down upon the tobacco fields were Oom Mias's wife and sons were hoeing, and there he was, smoking in the shade. He looked rather embarrassed to see me as he had always told everyone what a hard-working man he was.

He was tall, tough and wiry, with curly chestnut hair. His dress was simple: cord trousers, flannel shirt and *veldskoene* and an old soft hat upon his head. He was famous: he had a reputation for being the biggest liar and the laziest man in the entire district.

Oom Mias was a *bywoner*; he lived on a corner of somebody else's farm where he eked out a living by growing tobacco, most of which found its way into his own pipe. Ever smiling and easy-going, he was also a great storyteller. Most of his stories were fictitious but, over time, he began to believe them himself. Very similar to people who gaze too long into the mirror of Aramathaeus – they become lost in the pool and forget their purpose in life – so Oom Mias could no longer distinguish between truth and falsehood.

He greeted me and said that he was suffering from a bad headache and was just resting for a few minutes. I didn't say anything but thought that tobacco was surely not good for a headache. Then he proceeded to talk …

'We people that toil and sweat in the sun for a living cannot afford to be ill. My cure for illness is work. Last time I had flu, I worked it off in three days. I dragged myself to the lands that morning but as soon as I became hot, I felt better. So I worked hard throughout the whole day without stopping. Had I stopped, even for a minute, I would have broken down, so I just kept on. My clothes became wringing wet, but I carried on. My wife came to me, crying, and begged me to stop. She said I was going to die; the way I was working was mad and unnatural; she'd never seen me work like this in the twenty years of our marriage. I would not heed her; I just carried on. She came to me three times a day, giving me a little *dop*. I swallowed the *dop* and went on as before. And, believe me, within three days I had hoed an area that had taken my wife and three sons a week to do the previous year!

'My wife over there works like a young girl, although she has had 12 children! I trained her to work and now she cannot live without it! She never had a sickle or hoe in her hand before she married me, yet now she uses them better than any man, except me of course.

'You will be surprised to hear how she married me, for she was very beautiful, her father was a very rich man and there were many suitors. Amongst them was Koos Prinsloo, a well-to-do young farmer but as mean as dirt. He came courting Sannie because he heard the old man was going to give her a farm as a wedding present. It was not that he wanted to marry her for the farm you understand; it's just that he didn't know how else to get it! Sannie's mother preferred Koos because he flattered her all day and the old man knew that Koos was a wealthy farmer. But Sannie did not like Koos at all. However, the mother told the entire aspirant *vryers* that Sannie really liked Koos so, one by one, they stopped coming around. Then it was just Koos and me left. Koos started telling the mother all sorts of bad things about me – like I had no money and many other wicked lies – until she started hinting that I should not come around any more, even though the father still liked me.

'One day I was longing to see Sannie so I rode over, unsaddled my horse, and went in. There was nobody there. I sat and waited. Sannie eventually came through, weeping, and said that her father was desperately ill, close to death. Her mother had told Koos to go and fetch Mrs Smith, a woman who was very clever with herbs. The mother told Koos that if he did this he could marry Sannie. But Sannie had gone and hidden Koos's saddle to delay him. Then Sannie said that if *I* went to fetch Mrs Smith and she cured her father then *I* would get the credit.

'I ran for the stables, just in time to hear Koos's hoofs clattering away. My saddle was missing, so I jumped on bareback and galloped after him. After about a mile I caught him up. Grabbing his reins, I forced him to stop.

'"Neef, Koos," I said, "why did you steal my saddle?"

'"I did not steal your saddle; I merely borrowed it because I could not find mine," he replied.

'"I am going to take you to the police station on the next farm and have you locked away for theft," I told him.

'Koos saw I was deadly serious and became afraid.

'"I'll buy it from you, what is your price?" he asked.

'"Ten pounds!" I said, quick as you like.

'"Ten pounds?" he exclaimed, nearly falling from his horse. "It's not worth 10 shillings!"

'"Well, let's go to the station," I suggested.

'Koos bargained all the way up to 10 pounds. When we got to the station I said that because he wanted it so badly the price was now 10 pounds plus his saddle. And, if he haggled further, the price would increase! He went white and agreed. I got my 10 pounds.

'"Now, let me go. I am in a hurry," he demanded.

'"Not so fast, Koos," I said. "Tant Jacoba sent me with a message for you. Oom Willem died just after you left the house and she wishes you to ride around and break the news to the Lotters, Meintjies and Smalbergers. She said it is better that you go because you are almost one of the family. The funeral will be tomorrow afternoon."

'Koos rode off to the Lotters as fast as he could. I went to fetch Mrs Smith. Riding back to the farm with her that night I told her that I was sent to fetch the doctor in town, but, knowing how much better than the doctor she was, had come straight to her. I had a friend for life! I confided in her that I was an upright, hard-working young farmer whose only crime was poverty. I told her that Annie wanted to marry me, but that her mother favoured Koos Prinsloo.

'Arriving on the farm, Oom Willem's room was full of relations. Mrs Smith shooed them all out. She opened the windows for air, had the coffin taken from the room, said a small prayer and examined Oom Willem. She administered her medicines and, shortly thereafter, Oom Willem was fast asleep like a baby.

'She kept me in the room with her all the time. When Oom Willem awoke the next morning he was well on the way to recovery and he sang my praises to the whole family. That afternoon the Lotters, Meirings and Smalbergers all arrived. They were very angry with what they discovered, especially when Koos tried to blame me. They all laid into him. Oom Willem said, "Sannie, take this young man into the garden and show him the flowers; he is faint from nursing me all night."

'So, Sannie took me into the garden and we have been in Eden ever since!'

The true settlers

A few years ago I related the story of the very first settlers in Table Bay. These were not, as most people have been taught, Jan van Riebeeck and his merry men but a group of English convicts who were unceremoniously dumped on the shores of Table Bay forty years before Van Riebeeck. They all came to a very sticky end, the last of them returning to England and being hanged at Sandwich Green! However, there was a second group of unwilling settlers that landed in Table Bay before Van Riebeeck, and this is their story.

In the December of 1646, six years before Van Riebeeck's arrival, three VOC ships – the *Nieu Haerlem*, the *Olifant* and the *Schiedam* – left Batavia for the return voyage to the Netherlands. Encountering stormy seas, the *Haerlem* became separated from the other two and entered Table Bay on 25 March 1647. There was another ship anchored in the roadstead. The Chief Mate of the *Nieu Haerlem*, Claes Winckels, and several other crew members lowered a boat and went to identify the other ship.

In the meantime, as is the wont of the Cape weather, a strong south-easterly picked up, driving the *Nieu Haerlem* shoreward. Attempts were made to steer the ship using different sails, but in vain. All the storm anchors were put out – they dragged. They dragged until their cables broke. As she hit the heavy surf the *Haerlem* fired her cannons to indicate distress to the other ship in the bay, before foundering on the beaches of the place we today call Milnerton.

The following day, Winckels returned to the *Haerlem* to report that the other ship was the *Olifant*, which had arrived a few days earlier. The skipper of the *Olifant* came on board the *Haerlem* and, with boats from both ships, tried unsuccessfully to free the beached vessel. The crew of the *Haerlem* managed to reach shore in boats and on barrels, all except one poor carpenter who was unable to swim. The crew then started to construct a tent on the beach to accommodate the survivors. That same evening two English ships anchored in the bay.

For the next couple of days, with the help of the crews of the English ships and the *Olifant*, cargo – including camphor and cinnamon – was taken ashore. Forty lucky crew members of the *Haerlem* left on the English ships, bound for St Helena Island. From there they would be transferred to returning VOC ships, of which there were 150 plying their trade across the oceans of the world.

The remaining crew of the *Haerlem* began to build a fortification on a hill close to where the wreck lay. Made of recovered wood the structure was large enough to accommodate the 42 remaining people. It was under the joint command of Junior Merchant Leendert Jansz and Winckels. Their job was to recover as much as they could from the wreck and store it in the fortification, known as Zandenburch, or Sandy Castle. It was then that the last of the three ships from the original fleet, the *Schiedam*, dropped anchor in the bay.

During the first ten days of April, construction of the fortification continued. Fresh water, from one of the natural springs that fed into Salt River, was found. The survivors began exploring for local resources. It is hard to believe, when one looks at the area now, that they actually hunted there. In August 1647, three Dutch East India Company ships, on their outward-bound voyage, dropped anchor in the bay.

Commissioners arrived to inspect the fortifications and to salvage the cargo. Their observations give us a clear indication of the construction of the camp. They found a rectangular fortification situated on top of a steep sand dune with a gun platform on each corner, with cannon on each platform. The breastworks were 3–4 m high with sharp protruding sticks and, on the north-west side, there was another battery of three guns to offer additional protection from the local inhabitants. One notes with surprise that even at this stage, prior to the arrival of Van Riebeeck, the local inhabitants of the Cape were not pleased with the arrival, by necessity or not, of foreign people. Animosity was beginning to grow.

All this information is contained in the meticulously kept diary of Leendert Jansz, which even includes diligent reports of the prevailing weather conditions. It is unfortunate that the diary ends on 14 September 1647, when the survivors and the cargo were taken aboard a returning fleet and returned to Holland.

However, the 1649 *remonstrantie* presented to Dutch East India Company directors on the Cape survivors' experiences proved invaluable, suggesting that further relationships should be established with the indigenous people. The brief also served to indicate the potential of the Cape as a refreshment station and was detailed enough to make possible the preparation of a budget for the proposed settlement. Various aspects of life and conditions in the region were explored – fresh water, game, favourable climatic conditions and soil types are all mentioned. And it was this very report that led to Jan van Riebeeck's now historic arrival at the Cape of Good Hope.

Recently, evidence has emerged regarding artefacts found on the sea bed close to where the *Haerlem* sank. It is my sincere hope that this leads to a maritime archaeological excavation to search for the wreck, as this would throw much-needed light on an important episode in the early modern history of South Africa.

Thirst for the past

Not so many years ago a fellow historian and I were standing in a little antique shop, a place we would often pass on our numerous history-gathering trips into the country.

Over a period of time, we eventually got to know the old lady who looked after the shop during the week. She told me that when she was a little girl she used to live in a now forgotten town in the middle of the Free State. This was not an unusual situation, as many South Africans grew up in similar towns dotted all over the countryside, many of them flourishing in their time, usually thanks to gold or diamonds. We have often spoken about these little towns and their quaint stories: places like Lichtenburg, Christiana, Bloemhof, Steyndorp, Malmani and the like – all have their secrets to divulge. But now, when you go there, all that remains are the ghosts of the past roaming the ruins.

But the old lady's story was different. She recalled that when she was a child she and her sister were playing alongside the outside wall of their little house. Suddenly, the stick she was digging with hit something solid. Excitedly, the girls dug up this 'treasure'. What they had unearthed was a box with metal clasps. They quickly took it inside to their father. He opened the box and, inside the lid, found the initials 'J S' inscribed. The box also held an array of papers. He hurriedly closed the lid and said, 'These are some of the papers of the late Jannie Smuts, from when he was in this town during the Anglo-Boer War. Fearing that he might be captured by the Tommies, he buried them at the side of our house. Your grandfather fed and slept him here before Smuts continued on his campaign. It is not right, nor respectful, to fiddle with things of the dead. This box must be returned and you are all forbidden to go there or ever speak of this again. Is that understood?'

Suitably terrified and chastised, the girls waited inside until their father had reburied the box.

The lady went on to say that she had never spoken of this amazing incident up till now. But, recognising that we were two historians dedicated to preserving our country's past, she thought it only right that should break her silence.

We were, naturally, dumbfounded. So we sat down and started to take notes, carefully recording every detail of the story.

All this happened in the Free State town of Jagersfontein, where her elderly sister still lived – in the same house they were born in. After making telephone arrangements and packing spades, shovels and metal detectors we set off one Friday afternoon for the metropolis of Jagersfontein.

Jagersfontein was originally a farm belonging to one Evert Jager, a Griqua of mixed blood. Philippolis, the original home of Adam Kok, lies just to the south. Jager and his family had trekked here to escape the hated British rule of the colony. In 1856 Jager sold the farm to a C J Visser.

The first recorded diamond find in South Africa was in 1867. Just three years later, in 1870, diamonds were discovered on the Jagersfontein Farm. The place went berserk! Most people don't know that this find pre-dates Kimberley, which was only formed in 1873. This makes Jagersfontein, not Kimberley, the oldest diamond-mining town in the country. Another little-known fact is that the Jagersfontein mine produced the second-largest diamond on record – 'The Excelsior'.

The town was beautifully laid out with Edwardian and Victorian masterpieces; all the buildings with their broekielace trimmings and their *stoeps* to protect the interiors from the burning heat of the day. You would come back from the mine exhausted, undress and have a bath drawn (Jagersfontein was the first place in the country to have municipal water installed). The street had water pumps by 1912, where you would insert a 'Water Penny' to purchase three gallons of fresh water. Just think, prepaid water as far back as 1912! You would then saunter over to your favourite watering hole. There were no fewer than five hotels in that little town, all with their honky-tonk pianos blasting away. The music-hall girls that followed any rush were already firmly ensconced and nights would be drunk and sung away, all thoughts of the hard day's labour in the mine banished.

Kimberley was discovered and very rapidly began to overshadow our Jagersfontein. Though her 'Big Hole' was larger and deeper than the Kimberley hole, she did not produce the quantity of the Kimberley mines. Eventually the town was overshadowed and forgotten, like so many other places and events in our history. Go and walk her streets one day – you will sense the spirits of our country's forgotten past as I have done.

As for the box of Jannie Smuts – we never found it. We dug around the side of the old house and the small population of the town turned up *en masse* to see what the hell we were up to! Though the mythical box never materialised, sometime later I did discover that the house belonged to one Jakobus Smit and I think this may be whom the initials stood for. What the truth is, we will probably never know; it remains, like the box, buried in the past. But one thing remains important: I had the chance to walk the streets of a memory and for that I am grateful.

A historical swindle

An entertaining story emerges from our country's illustrious past. Its themes of greed and corruption are, sadly, still relevant today; which just goes to show that not much changes with the march of time.

The year 1886 sees the discovery of gold on the Witwatersrand. Everyone is stunned by the enormity of the estimated wealth buried there – when people talk about it their eyes glaze over. Then, four years later, the Transvaal Republic announces, 'A vast new Goldfield!' The world is again captivated. The dusty little town of Leydsdorp in the north is to become this area's new capital. There follows an even more surprising announcement: the area is to have its own railway line! Surprising, because the region has no decent roads to speak of, never mind a railway!

People with any knowledge of railway construction realised that something must be seriously amiss. When they estimated the costs involved, then measured these against the total (small) population of the Lowveld at the time, they realised that somebody in the Volksraad in Pretoria had gone absolutely mad. Well, the Volksraad member behind this madness was a Mr B J Vorster, a personal friend of President Kruger's. Barend Vorster and his friends had surmised that when the railway line connecting Pretoria and Delagoa Bay was completed it would not be difficult to put through a branch line running from Komatiepoort to the new Selati goldfields the output of which, everybody said, would dwarf that of the Witwatersrand. The Portuguese had already completed their part from Delagoa Bay to the border (although, in fairness, this was the easier section) but it was not until 1894 that the Pretoria link-up would occur.

Vorster and two associates, Porcheron and Stephenson, petitioned the Volksraad for the concession to build the railway line. The Volksraad favoured their bid over other, more solid, company tenders, as it was customary then for the Transvaal Republic to award concessions to Burgers first. Well knowing that they did not have the required capital to finance the deal, however, the Volksraad stipulated that the concession could not be sold to a British Company since they considered there were enough English-speaking people in the Transvaal already. But Vorster and his colleagues were so sure of securing the concession that they had already sold it on, before the Volksraad had ratified the deal!

Now, onto the Transvaal stage comes one of life's real characters – a Frenchman, Baron Eugene Oppenheim. He is a mere 22 years of age, but so impresses Vorster and associates that they sell him the concession for £80 000 plus one twentieth of the capital of the company to be formed. The plot begins to thicken …

Baron Eugene had decided on the company's name – wait for it – La Compagnie Franco-Belge du Chemin-de-fer du Nord de la Republique Sud-Africaine. The French Oppenheim was going to establish his headquarters in Belgium because there were more loopholes in company law there than in France!

We will never know why Vorster and his friends decided to negotiate with this young 22-year-old. What we do know is that Oppenheim arrives in Pretoria just before the awarding of the contract by the Volksraad and hosts a huge banquet at the Transvaal Hotel in the city. Everybody who is anybody is invited. The Baron pays £300 for a portrait in oils of President Kruger, to be hung in the Volksraad. He gives away gold watches and spider carriages to members of the Raad; he spends another £6 500 of his own money on "Commissions to principal members of the Executive Council, and the Legislative Assembly, with a view to obtaining the provisional concession". He says later that he also had to pay the President £4 000. Subsequent investigations prove the Baron to be a liar of the first order, although lavish gifts were given to members of the Volksraad. It was also discovered that the Baron's company at no time had the stipulated £500 000 to finance the deal.

Oppenheim's plan was to enter into a contract with one Louis Warnant to build the line at a maximum cost of £9 600 per mile, which was the amount allowed by the government. Warnant was then to enter into a sub-contract with a British engineering firm that was willing to build the line at £7 000 per mile. The total cost of the contract allowed was £1 848 000, as opposed to the £1 348 000 (payable at £7 000 per mile) Oppenheim's scam involved. This would give the Baron a tidy profit of £500 000. He then cooks the books of the company to show that the capital is in place and begins drawing the 4% interest that the government of the Republic has guaranteed!

Thank goodness then for Mr J M Smit, the Railways Commissioner, who uncovered the swindle. Thus exposed, Baron Eugene Oppenhiem, Henri Warnant and their lawyer are charged and found guilty in the Belgian criminal courts. They are fined and sent to prison, though not before they have ruined the contracting firm and cost share and debenture holders thousands of pounds.

So the Northern Railway became a line to nowhere. It was laid from Komatiepoort to just before Skukuza Camp in the Kruger National Park. And, all along the way, the line was strewn with picks, shovels, sleepers and impedimenta, which were to lie there and rust – the railway line would only be completed twenty years later.

As for the Selati goldfields, they never lived up to people's vast expectations and the bustling new capital slipped back to being a sleepy little hollow in the Lowveld. So much for the dreams of mice and men!

God's finger

The theatre of war always seems to be acted out in extremes. The extremes of cruelty yet also the extremes of human love and understanding, as this poignant story demonstrates.

'Call the roll, sergeant,' said the British Officer, as the Boer POWs lined up to answer to their names.

'Basson – Ja.'

The sergeant continued the roll call, 'Beyers, Brink, De Jong, Dominee.'

Once they had answered the men ceased to be there; their minds and attentions elsewhere, in dreams of their wives and children, their homes and their cattle and the memories of a war that was lost. But Jan Moolman had other ideas. Tomorrow, he would vanish. He'd already organised the substitute answerer for the morning roll call, when no head-count was made.

Moolman was a renowned hunter amongst his people and, with his beloved Francina now dead, there were only three things that he loved: his country, his hunting and his horses. There was nothing and nobody he hated except the English, after they started burning the farms and taking the wives and the children into what they termed 'protective custody', protection that saw them die the way a caged wild bird would – of a broken heart.

He made his escape, and, with the patience that only a hunter has, lay in his lair all day as they searched for him. You see, Jan Moolman had hidden away inside the camp, not outside where everyone expected him to be. For three days he stayed hidden, living off the bare provisions that he'd kept for just this occasion. That third night he made his break for the world outside. Overpowering a sentry and disguising himself in his British uniform, Moolman stole a horse and saddle and set out for the mountains, saluted by the guard on gate-duty as he left. Once in the Waterberg he would be safe, unless his own people shot him – believing him to be a British cavalry officer.

He rode past gutted farmhouses, their lifeless windows staring out of broken walls like the eye sockets of a dead man's skull. They said it was done with kindness – if one can burn a man's house and take his cattle kindly, if it is possible to abduct his family with gentleness. No, they had done it to break the heart and the soul of a nation. Jan had ridden about 80 km when he found a place that he liked the look of: a burnt-out house with beautiful views in all directions. He could see who was coming and if he had to run he would have a good start. Moolman hobbled his horse and went inside to explore. The house held nothing but the charred remains of furniture and fallen thatch. But in one room he was astounded to discover a woman lying on the floor, with a child sitting beside her.

'So you are back,' she said. 'What do you want now? There is nothing left to take and nothing more to burn. Why don't you just leave and let us die in our house. And bring the others; bring them all to see a Boer woman die.'

'*Nee*', he said, 'I am not English *Mevrou* – I am a Boer who has escaped. I am Jannie Moolman.'

'Moolman,' the woman said, 'the man with a price on his head? The man who blew up the bridge at Klipdrift?'

'*Ja* – and you're starving.'

'Yes,' she said, 'won't you bring us some water, we can no longer walk – we can't even stand.'

She pointed to a tin cup and he returned with some water for her and the child.

'We have no food *Meneer*, but if you lift the floorboards in the kitchen there is a rifle and some ammunition.'

Moolman left to hunt, after changing back into Boer clothes that had been hidden in a nearby cave. From a small herd of springbok he brought down a nice buck and headed back to the farmhouse. The next day, both were stronger – the little girl was on her feet and the mother could sit up.

'You must go on,' she said, 'We can manage now.'

'I cannot leave you with food for two days with no salt – the meat will go off. No, I have made up my mind: I will stay and hunt until you can travel, then you must ride my horse and we will all go into the mountains,' Jannie said.

'That will take time,' the woman replied.

'*Ja*,' he said, 'it will take time, but I have time. I have all the time in the world. You see *Mevrou*, time and the air and the water are the only things that cost nothing. They are the gifts of God.'

'You are the gift of God, *Meneer.*'

The woman's name was Jacoba de Wet. She had blue eyes and blonde hair and was no older than 25, and the child was a miniature version of her. The days passed and the woman and the child recovered completely.

One day the little girl came running in, shouting, 'Men are coming – men on horses.'

Jan went to the door and saw a detachment of British Lancers approaching. They were so near you could hear the rattle and the clash of their equipment. Jan Moolman adjusted his hat, smoothed his tailcoat and went to meet them. A young officer rode forward. Jan took off his hat and greeted him politely.

'Sir,' he said in English, 'I never thought I would welcome one of your race. But times change and, being perceptive, I change with those times. In the house lie a sick child and woman. They need tea, bread and sugar.'

'You speak English well,' said the officer.

'Yes,' Jan said, 'I had the good fortune to be educated.'

'I am going inside,' said the officer 'Corporal Brown, bring two men.'

The soldiers all carried carbines.

'Enter,' said Moolman, 'we can offer you little hospitality. Partly because you are the enemy, but mainly because you have destroyed the woman's possessions.'

'We saw smoke,' the officer said, 'and smoke to the British is like honey to a bee. This area is supposed to be cleared.'

'Ja, *Meneer*,' said Jan, 'that is one word. Devastated is another.'

The officer looked at the springbok hanging.

'Someone shot it with that Mauser,' he said, looking at the rifle that Jacoba was desperately trying to hide. Then he looked at Jan again.

'I have seen you somewhere before. Slim, 5' 7", dark eyes. Talks English very well. Moustache. By God!' the officer exclaimed 'You're Moolman!'

The officer ordered his men to arrest Moolman, informing him that he would be shot if they found the British uniform he'd escaped in. Jan, however, remained cool under pressure and calmly told the officer of his role in helping the woman and child regain strength in order that the three of them might escape to the mountains.

'Moolman,' the officer said, 'I do not like this business, many of us don't. We are soldiers, we do not like burning farms, deporting women and children and stealing stock. If I let you go, will you give your word that you will not fight against us again?'

Jan looked at the man, 'If you took me, I should not be able to fight, so I will say yes.'

'Very well,' the officer replied, 'I cannot let you go, but you might manage to escape with the woman and the child. Could you steal a second horse?'

'*Ja*, I could do that,' said Jan.

'And if some rations were left out by mistake, could you steal those too?'

'*Meneer* – I am an expert thief,' said Moolman.

He went back to Jacoba to tell her that the officer was going to let them escape that night.

'Why, Jan?' she asked.

'Because he is a good man and he sees in this the finger of God. He is sick of the destruction and perhaps wants to make up for some of the harm that he has done.'

'*Ja*, Jan,' she said, 'in this I also see the finger of God and who am I to turn away when he points?'

That night, they were gone.

'She who walks by moonlight'

We in this country of European leanings have grown up with the folk tales of Hans Christian Andersen and Aesop's Fables, to name but two childhood influences. These stories were written to expound certain moral standards and values for people to adhere to and, if they did, their society would function more smoothly. The mythology and morality tales that have been passed down from generation to generation in Africa are equally fascinating. One of these fables is about Sihamba-Ngenyanga – 'she-who-walks-by-moonlight'.

In the story Sihamba-Ngenyanga grows into a beautiful woman; she represents the beauty of Nature in the female form. She is a blessing to all of society. Such beauty must therefore be protected, for to abuse it is to negate it and the happiness engendered by that beauty will therefore be lost. It is man's privilege to gaze upon Sihamba-Ngenyanga. But people are punished when they attempt to assign inappropriate functions to the girl. Beauty, when violated, returns to its source – Mother Nature – as we shall discover in this wonderful Xhosa legend …

There once was a very wealthy man who had many wives, including one who was very beautiful. In the beginning the beautiful one was the man's favourite and this, of course, made the co-wives very jealous. Unfortunately, as time passed, it became apparent that she could bear no children. This disappointed her husband greatly. After a while she lost his attention and he began to neglect, then eventually despise, her. She became the laughing stock of the co-wives. The other women formed themselves into working groups, hoeing fields and cutting grass together, but they would not work with her. She worked alone. Many moons would come and go without her even seeing her husband. She found herself constantly in tears and her beauty began to fade.

One day she went, as usual, to hoe the field. She worked hard to release her pain and the tears streamed down her cheeks.

'Why are you crying *nkosikazi*? What makes you so sad?' said a voice.

The speaker was one of two doves that had perched on the bough of a nearby tree.

'I am sad because I have lost the love of my man, for I cannot bear him children,' the woman replied.

Without another word the doves flew off only to return a short time later with two pellets in their beaks, which they gave to the woman to eat. The woman swallowed the pellets eagerly then offered some corn to the doves in thanks, which they refused.

Sure enough, after several moons, she became heavy with child. She made up her mind to tell nobody about this marvellous occurrence. And, as nobody visited her, no one would notice the difference. She gave birth to a girl of exceptional beauty and named her Thanga-Limlibo (budding little pumpkin). Resenting her husband's behaviour the woman resolved to keep the child hidden. So she never took Thanga-Limlibo outside during the day, only at night. However, when the girl reached puberty her mother allowed her to perform several chores in and around the courtyard during the daytime. The villagers noticed this new, lovely girl in their midst and they were dumbstruck – her beauty was such that they just stood and gazed at her. The men would not go hunting. The women would not go and hoe the fields. The girls would not go and draw water from the spring. The herd boys would not drive the cattle and goats to the pastures; even the animals were captivated. All living things simply flocked to the courtyard to behold the girl.

News of the entrancing young woman reached the ears of the headman, her father, who immediately set out to investigate. He was staggered to find his wife beautiful once more, her looks restored through love of her precious child. He embraced the daughter and begged forgiveness from the mother for the years of cruelty he'd inflicted on her. He then set about preparing a great feast in honour of Thanga-Limlibo.

Now that Thanga-Limlibo had been seen by the people and recognised by her father, it was not necessary to keep her indoors any more. But herein lay the problem. If she went to draw water from the spring, everybody followed her; if she was working about the house, people stood transfixed and would not move until she went inside. And so the people decided that because her beauty disrupted the natural rhythm of the community she was only to come out by moonlight; in this way, the work of the village could continue uninterrupted. Those who wanted to could watch her after sunset, as she went about her duties by the light of the moon. She therefore became known as Sihamba-Ngenyanga – 'she-who-walks-by-moonlight'.

At the honouring feast Sihamba-Ngenyanga met a handsome young man and it soon became known that they were to marry. Following the marriage, the villagers told the husband and his family that in her new home the custom of keeping Sihamba-Ngenyanga inside during the day should continue to be strictly enforced. Her new family heeded this advice: the lovely maiden only came out at night to hoe the fields and draw water from the river. The people knew this and they would come and gaze at her as she passed by.

In time, a baby was born to the couple. An *impelesi* (young nursemaid) was sent to look after the infant. At that time there also stayed in the house with Sihamba-Ngenyanga a withered old woman. She was the mother of her father-in-law and so worn with age that she could nothing for herself; whoever remained in the house with her had to fulfil all her needs.

In the middle of one particular day the old woman became thirsty. Sihamba-Ngenyanga brought her some water but she complained that it was sour and demanded fresh, immediately. Sihamba-Ngenyanga reminded her that there was no one to bring this, as the river was rather far and the *impelesi* too young to go there alone. The crone replied, 'I can't die of thirst when there is a grown woman in the house. Go and fetch me fresh water at once!'

'She-who-walks-by-moonlight' picked up her pot and ladle and stepped into the light of day to go and draw water. Though she knew the way well by moonlight, the bright sunlight dazzled and confused her. She stumbled and fell several times on her way, but eventually reached the river.

As she tried to draw water with the calabash ladle it was pulled out of her hand by some unseen force and disappeared into the water. She tried to draw with the water pot; this too was pulled out of her hands and disappeared. She took off her leather mantle to try to draw water but this was also wrenched from her grasp. In desperation, Sihamba-Ngenyanga took off her head cover and dipped it into the water, hoping to run back home and let the thirsty old woman suck on it. This too was taken from her. In one last effort she cupped her hands to draw just sufficient water to wet the throat of the old woman. The unseen force drew her under the water's surface and she disappeared.

When everybody returned from the fields the *impelesi* told them what had happened. The adults saw her footmarks at the water's edge and feared the worst. After searching everywhere for her they were forced to admit that Sihamba-Ngenyanga must have drowned. Meanwhile, the baby was hungry and crying for its mother.

At moonrise that night the *impelesi* picked up the baby and, without saying a word, walked to the place where the mother had vanished. And while she stood there she sang sadly, calling to the mother:

'*Uyalila, Uyalila, Sihamba-Ngenyanga*
Uyalila umntan'akho. Uyalila.
Kha uphume umanyise, Sihamba-Ngenyanga
Sihamba-Ngenyanga.'

'It is crying, it is crying, Sihamba-Ngenyanga
It is crying. Your baby is crying, come out and suckle it.'

There was a disturbance on the surface of the river and the mother appeared, standing breast high in its flow. Sihamba-Ngenyanga sang back:

'It was intentional; they sent me to draw water during the daytime.
I tried the pot, it sank,
I tried the mantle, it sank,
I tried the head cover and it sank,
And when I drew with my hands, I sank.'

Then she came out of the water and took the baby in her arms and suckled it. After the child had fed she handed it back to the *impelesi* without a word and slipped back into the river once more. The *impelesi* carried the baby home and put it to bed, but returned the following nights to repeat the same ritual. After a while, the in-laws became suspicious of her curious behaviour and questioned her. The *impelesi* told them what had been happening. The men decided to waylay the mother, thinking they would grab hold of her when she next appeared. So, before moonrise, they hid themselves in the reeds near the river and waited. They saw the *impelesi* come with the baby and heard her sing her sad song. They saw Sihamba-Ngenyanga standing breast high in the water, heard her song and saw her suckle and caress the child. Just as the infant was about to be returned to its nursemaid the men sprang forward and took hold of Sihamba-Ngenyanga.

However, as they carried her home, they saw to their horror that the river came after them. Beyond the reeds it followed, then through the woods, then up the slope and right into the village. The people were petrified and they put Sihamba-Ngenyanga down. Immediately, the river took hold of her and receded. The people were at a loss to understand the meaning of this. The two doves then appeared and offered to fly to Sihamba-Ngenyanga's own people to seek advice. The villagers accepted. On reaching Sihamba-Ngenyanga's family village the doves perched on the posts of the cattle kraal. Seeing them, the herd boys sprang forward, thinking to kill and eat the pair. But, just in time, the doves sang out:

'We are not the doves that may be killed
For we come to tell of Sihamba-Ngenyanga.

She dipped the ladle and it sank,
She dipped the pot and it sank,
She dipped the mantle and it sank,
She dipped her hands,
And she sank.'

A message came back with the doves instructing the people to slaughter and flay the beautiful dung-coloured ox that was the leading ox of Sihamba-Ngenyanga's *lobola*, then throw the carcass in the water. The order was executed immediately. At moonrise that night, when the *impelesi* carried the baby to the water's edge, all the people of the village followed. They heard her sing her sad song. They saw Sihamba-Ngenyanga standing breast high in the water. They heard the mother sing her song and watched as she came out to suckle and fondle her child. Except this time the mother did not hand the baby back to the *impelesi*; instead she carried it lovingly in her own arms and walked quietly back to the village with the others.

The wrong had been repaired; order and balance were restored to the village once more. Such are the stories of Africa.

Bibliography

Barnard, Lady Anne. 1908. *South Africa a Century ago*. Smith, Elder and Company, UK.

Benade, Thérèse. 2004. *Kites of Good Fortune*. David Philip, Cape Town.

Biggs, David. 2004. *Karoo Ramblings*. Struik, Cape Town.

Bloomhill, Greta. 1962. *Witchcraft in Africa*. Howard B. Timmins, Cape Town.

Brownley, The Honourable Chas. 1896. *Reminiscences of Kaffir Life and History*. Lovedale Mission Press, South Africa

Bulpin, T.V. 1955. *Storm over the Transvaal*. Howard B. Timmins, Cape Town.

Bulpin, T.V. 1970. *Discovering South Africa*. Tafelberg, Cape Town.

Cartwright, A.P. 1974. *By the waters of the Letaba*. Purnell, London.

Cloete, Stuart. 1974. *South of Capricorn*. Academia, Cape Town.

Couzens, Tim. 2004. *Battles of South Africa*. David Philip, Cape Town.

Crampton, Hazel. 2004. *The Sunburnt Queen*. Jacana Media, Johannesburg.

De Kock, Victor. 1950. *Those in Bondage*. Howard B. Timmins, Cape Town.

Du Preez, Max. 2004. *Of Warriors, Lovers and Prophets*. Zebra Press, Cape Town.

Elliott, Aubrey. 1975. *The Magic World of the Xhosa*. Collins, London.

Fraser, J.G. and Briggs, James. 1985. *Sotho War Diaries*. Human and Rousseau, Cape Town.

Fuller, Basil. 1962. *Springbok round the corner*. Maskew Miller Limited, Cape Town.

Gordon, Lady Duff. 1927. *Letters from the Cape*. Oxford University Press, London.

Green, Lawrence G. 1957. *Beyond the City Lights*. Howard B. Timmins, Cape Town.

Green, Lawrence G. 1985. *The Best of Lawrence G. Green* – Edited by Maureen Barnes. Penguin Books, London.

Green, Lawrence. G. 1960. *Eight bells of Salamander*. Howard B. Timmins, Cape Town.

Harrington, A.L. 1980. *Sir Harry Smith: Bungling Hero*. Tafelberg Publishers Limited, Cape Town.

Hugo, Leon and Betty. 1974. *South of Capricorn*. Academica, Pretoria.

James, Allan. 2001. *The First Bushman's Path*. University of Natal Press, Pietermaritzburg.

Jeal, Tim. 1973. *Livingstone*. Pimlico, London.

Jordaan, A.C. 1973. *Tales from Southern Africa*. AD Donker, Johannesburg.

Krige, Uys. 1945. *The way out*. Unpublished.

Ladysmith Historical Society. 1972. *The Smiths of Ladysmith and Harrismith*.

McCord, Margaret. 2000. *The Calling of Katie Makanya*. David Philip, Cape Town.

Millin, Sarah Gertrude. *King of the Bastards*. Windmill Press, UK.

Molema, S.M. 1966. *Montshiwa*. Struik Limited, Cape Town.

Monnig, H.O. 1967. *The Pedi*. Van Schaik Limited, Pretoria.

Mostert, Noel. 1993. *Frontiers*. Pimlico, London.

Mountain, Alan. 2004. *An unsung heritage*. David Philip, Cape Town.

Muller, Professor Ampie and Bev Ross. Unpublished work. Rosebank, Cape Town.

Mutwa, V.C. 1966. *Africa is my Witness*. Blue Crane Books, Johannesburg

Partridge, A.C. 1973. *Volklaw of Southern Africa*. Purnell, Johannesburg.

Peires, Jeff. 1981. *The house of Phalo*. Jonathan Ball Publishers, Cape Town.

Peters, Dr Carl. 1902. *The Eldorado of the Ancients*. C Arthur Pearson Limited, UK.

Schapera, I. 1953. *The Bantu Speaking Peoples of South Africa*. Maskew Miller Limited, Cape Town.

Schoeman, P.J. 1957. *Hunters of the Desert Land*. Howard B. Timmins, Cape Town.

Shillington, Kevin. 1985. *The Colonisation of the Southern Tswana 1870–1900*. Ravan Press, Johannesburg.

Sonntag, Christopher. 1918. *My Friend Malaboch Chief of the Blue Mountains*. Sigma Press, Pretoria.

Stapelton, Timothy J. 1994. *Maqoma Xhosa Resistance to the Colonial Advance*. Jonathan Ball Publishers, Cape Town.

Summers, Roger. 1969. *Ancient Mining in Rhodesia and Adjacent Areas*. National Museum of Rhodesia.

Taylor, Stephen. 2004. *The Caliban Shore*. Faber and Faber, London.

Teale, G.M. 1916. *South Africa*. Maskew Miller, London, UK.

The Eastern Cape Naturalist no 59, 1976.

Turkington, Kate. 1983. *The South Wind and the Sun*. De Jager, Johannesburg.

Van Riebeek Society Cape Town. 1971. *Descriptions of the Cape of Good Hope with matters concerning it* (Volumes 1 and 2). Van Riebeek Society, Cape Town.

Walker, Michael. 2002. *Kalk Bay*. Michael Walker, Cape Town.

Wannenburgh, Alf. 1967. *Forgotten Frontiersmen*. Howard B. Timmins, Cape Town.

Wongtschowski, Brigett. 2003. *Between Woodbush and Wolkberg*. Protea Book House, Pretoria.